On a
yo

Whispers
From
Heaven

Dayle Allen Shockley

Pacific Press Publishing Association
Boise, Idaho
Oshawa, Ontario, Canada

Edited by Jerry D. Thomas
Designed by Dennis Ferree
Stained-glass art by Michael C. Booth
Typeset in 12/16 New Century Schoolbook

Library of Congress Cataloging-in-Publication Data:

Shockley, Dayle Allen, 1955-
    Whispers from heaven : on an ordinary day you can hear / Dayle
Allen Shockley.
        p.   cm.
    ISBN 0-8163-1237-0
    1. Meditations. 2. Shockley, Dayle Allen, 1955- I. Title.
BV4801.S46 1994
242—dc20   94-27730
                                                          CIP

TABLE OF CONTENTS

WHISPERS FROM HEAVEN

DEDICATION

This book is lovingly dedicated to my parents,
Rev. A. L. and Ruth K. Allen.
Because you planted me firmly in the fertile soil of truth,
I have never been uprooted by the storms of life.
I love you.

ACKNOWLEDGMENTS

I owe so much to so many:

To the Lord of my life, Jesus Christ. I could not write one complete sentence without the inspiration He so freely gives.

To the book editors at Pacific Press for their belief in my abilities and for their patience with me as I wrote my first book.

To my only living grandparent, Thomas Ray Kynerd. You taught me how to genuinely treasure the written Word of God.

To my sister Elaine Fauss and her husband David. No matter what dream I chased, you both always cheered me on, helping me believe I could accomplish whatever I set out to do.

To my twin sister Gayle Cox and her husband Charles. Thanks

for propping me up when I wanted to quit. You gave me the courage to keep going in the midst of a difficult season.

To my circle of loyal encouragers, Amy Griffin, Susan Mondragon, Juanita Wigginton, and Cindy Miller. I always thank God for you.

To my mother-in-law, Mildred Shockley. You have stood firm in the face of great adversities. Your rock-solid faith now lives in my husband.

To my pastor, Orlin R. Fauss. Not only do you preach an undiluted message, you also step on my toes and send me to my knees. Please don't ever change.

To my wonderful church family at Bethel Tabernacle in Houston, Texas. You are my brothers and sisters.

To those who so willingly shared their stories with me. Thank you for letting me share them with our fellow travelers.

But most of all, to my lovely daughter Anna Marie, who opens my eyes to so much and makes my life a bouquet of sweet fragrances. And to my dear husband Stan, who knows all my shortcomings, yet loves me completely. I will love you both forever.

Wise men aren't always silent, but they know when to be.
Anonymous

The Unexpected Messenger

On a brisk day in April, my husband and I stood in the middle of the living-room floor, arguing. We seemed to be doing little else lately. I don't recall what started the whole thing; probably something as insignificant as who left the closet light on. Still, I rambled on, making little, if any, sense. My husband's face remained a picture of sheer frustration.

At last I announced, with great emphasis, "I'm getting out of here!"

"Go," Stan said, shrugging his broad shoulders. "Do whatever you want to do." He turned and walked away.

Still muttering, I stomped to the pantry, grabbed an old loaf of bread, stalked to the car, and drove to the duck pond.

This particular duck pond sits twelve miles from our home, in the center of the cemetery where my father-in-law is buried. For some reason, the pond has become a compass to me during difficult times. Maybe it held an answer today.

WHISPERS FROM HEAVEN

A parade of squawking ducks waddled to greet me. While I reached into the back seat for my sweater and the things I'd brought, they nosed around my feet, searching for whatever treats they could find.

"Just old bread, you guys," I said, shooing them out of the way.

The entire congregation trailed me to the small cement bench next to the pond. Hungrily, they eyed me as I unwrapped my meager offering. In minutes, the crumbs were consumed, and I silently enjoyed the pleasant breeze as the ducks sashayed off in every direction.

For a while, I sat under the Texas pines thinking about the argument I'd walked out on. All my life I'd heard the seventh year of marriage was the toughest; that men and women often contracted the seven-year-itch or something similar. I dared not define my own ailment, except to acknowledge that my marriage had tarnished over the years. The reasons varied, but my tendency to drone on when enough had been said didn't help matters. I always wanted to have the last word—at any cost.

Often I vowed to be different, spending weeks with Ecclesiastes 3:7—a time to speak and a time to be silent—taped on my bathroom mirror. But before long, I'd find myself stuck in the same old rut: talking when silence was in order. Inwardly, I longed for change.

Getting up from where I sat, I strolled to the edge of the pond, watching the ducks in the water creating spectacular silver circles around them, their reflections a kaleidoscope of colors.

If only I could behold my own reflection like the ducks in the water, I thought. *If only I could see myself.* And so I breathed a silent prayer, asking God to let this miraculous thing happen.

It was while I prayed that a car approached the little pond. Stopping a dozen feet from where I stood, the engine sputtered a time or two, then died. Turning, I saw an elderly man crawling out of an ancient, ramshackle Cadillac, the vinyl roof peeling off in great chunks.

Tall and lean, the man moved briskly around the front of the car, swinging two loaves of white Wonder bread in his hands He wore a red flannel shirt, sleeves clasped at the wrist, and jean britches, about an inch too short.

Hurriedly he laid the bags of bread on the hood of the Cadillac, opened them, and began flinging whole slices through the dazzling sun, like tiny white frisbees.

"You come here often?" I called out across the grass.

He cupped a hand to one ear.

"Do you come here often?" I said, a bit louder.

Tossing the final slices, he stuffed the plastic wrappers in a garbage bin and walked to where I now sat on the bench.

"I'm sorry, ma'am," he said, squatting beside me. "I still didn't hear you."

"I just wanted to know if you come here often," I said, suddenly wishing I hadn't said anything.

WHISPERS FROM HEAVEN

"I come when the weather's nice," he said. I found it unnerving that he did not look directly into my eyes when he spoke but stared curiously at my forehead.

For nothing better to do, we sat together on the bench, a cluster of ducks gathering at our feet, honking at a lofty volume. So loud was their honking that I had to resist the urge to jump up and yell, "SHHHH!" at the top of my lungs.

I glanced at the old man. He smiled but said nothing. I wished he would leave.

As if reading my mind, the man sprang to his feet and said, "I gotta split." Then he pointed a bony finger at the chattering ducks, and, in an irked voice, said, "You know, them crazy ducks just don't know when to hush."

With that declaration—and a wave in my direction—the old man sauntered to the waiting jalopy, brought it to life, and clanked off in the distance, a flurry of leaves chasing after him.

With a bewildered face, I stared at the disappearing car. What did he say? Suddenly, it seemed like a light bulb turned on in my head. *Did he say those crazy ducks just don't know when to hush?*

At once, I recalled my prayer, my desire to see myself. *Did God propel me to this place to catch a unique glimpse of myself?* I wondered. *Did I sound much like the honking ducks?* Suddenly, I knew I did. And I had the uncanny feeling that I had just entertained an angel.

Turning abruptly, I hurried to the car, a gust of April's wind whipping around my legs. The little ducks stood quiet now, like tiny monuments scattered across the ground. Their silence spoke volumes to me.

When I arrived home, my husband lay sprawled on the couch, looking worried. "Hi," he said, his voice even. "Where've you been?"

I hesitated briefly. "I went to the cemetery."

"Cemetery!" He half laughed. "Are you planning on killing me?"

"Nope," I said, planting a kiss on his puzzled face, "but I sure got some great pointers on keeping you alive."

"A quarrelsome wife is like a constant dripping on a rainy day."
(Proverbs 27:15, NIV)

O God, help me tame my tongue.

The head begins to swell when the mind stops growing.
Anonymous

Watch Your Step

t had been a good month. I delighted in see-ing my work in four different publications—all in the same month—and a contract lay on my desk for a piece I had peddled longer than I cared to remember. Not only that, there were other manu-scripts circulating in the mail; I felt certain they'd sell.

Calling it a celebration of success, I decided to go on a shop-ping spree. Nothing exorbitant. Just hit a few shops on my side of town. After all, I reasoned, I deserved it.

Pulling on a favorite blouse and skirt, I caught a glimpse of myself in the full-length mirror. Wow! I simply glowed. Falling perfectly across my shoulders, my chestnut hair never looked better; my outfit, crisp and stunning. Maybe I'd even lost a pound or two. Feeling like a million dollars, I adjusted my shoulder pads and breezed out of the room, anxious for the day's rewards.

It was an afternoon made in heaven. Everywhere I turned, sale signs appeared. Hours later, I drove home feeling richer than when I left. In fact, I couldn't remember when I had felt so good about myself.

Back inside the house, I sorted through the mail scattered across the kitchen table. There was one piece for me, which I opened immediately. It read: *We are sorry, but your submission does not meet our editorial needs at this time. Please try again in the future.* The letter was signed, "The Editors." I hated these form letters. So cold and unfeeling. Tossing the bad news on my desk, I resisted the sudden urge to stick my tongue out at it.

Just then, my daughter rounded the corner, making the usual inquiry; "Hi, Mom! D'ya buy me somethin'?"

"No, baby. Mommy didn't buy you anything today."

"What's this?" she asked.

"This is something I bought for myself."

"No. *This*," she said, touching the back of my left shoulder.

"What, Anna?"

"Just go look in the mirror, Mom," she said, perturbed.

Gathering my purchases, I marched down the hall and checked my appearance in the bathroom mirror. Horrified, my mouth flew open. It seemed that at some point during the afternoon jaunt, my left shoulder pad had become restless and now dangled precariously behind my back.

Who saw me like this? I wondered, my face blushing at the thought. *How could I not have noticed it?* How embarrassing!

Realizing it must have happened while trying on one of a dozen outfits, I stuffed the wayward pad back in place and stared at my gloomy reflection, my vanity totally squashed. First the rejection letter; now this mortifying experience.

All at once, I burst out laughing. What was it that Jesus said about the person who exalts himself being sure to be humbled?

I could almost hear the Lord saying, "Gotcha!"

"Whosoever shall exalt himself shall be abased; and he that shall humble himself shall be exalted."
(Matthew 23:12, KJV)

Thank You, God, for deflating me in my puffed-up moments. Never let me forget that I am nothing without You.

Thou that hast given so much to me, give one thing more—a grateful heart.
George Herbert

Counting Blessings

om!" my daughter—then four—calls to me from her bedroom. Quickly, I place the eggs in the pot of water, turn the burner on high, and head down the hall.

In her room, Anna sits propped up on a pile of pillows, looking sleepy eyed. Naptime.

"What's up?" I ask her.

"You read me a story?"

"OK, but just one. Mommy's boiling eggs."

She nods. Together, we nestle down between the cool sheets, strips of yellow sunshine streaming through the blinds. Halfway through the book, her eyes droop, and she yawns, slipping farther down into the covers. In minutes, she's napping peacefully.

The eggs forgotten, I curl up next to her and drift off.

About an hour later, a putrid smell beckons me to the kitchen. An empty, dry pot smokes above a red burner, and—to my hor-

ror—the eggs have exploded!

Everywhere I look, pieces of blackened egg lay scattered. There is egg on the floor, egg on the cabinets, egg on the ceiling, egg on the countertops. There is even egg in the adjacent room! What an awful mess!

Muttering, I reach for the broom, begin swiping at the splotches of egg on the ceiling, then crawl up on the counter to get a better aim. It is while I work that Anna strolls in, holding her nose.

"Yuck! Whasat I smell?" she asks. Upon seeing me, she gasps, "Mom, what on *earf* happened?"

With as little enthusiasm as possible, I relate the entire story, ending with, "Look at this mess! I am just *sick!*" My voice rises with hysteria.

Her answer is sobering. "Well, you oughta be happy," she scolds, her little face stern.

I glare down at her, speechless. Happy?

"It coulda burned our house all down. Couldn't it, Mama?" she says, her brown eyes piercing mine. She isn't finished. "It coulda burned us up too! That would make Daddy so sad. Wouldn't it, Mama?"

Climbing down from my perch, I wonder how on earth I ever got along without such wisdom. Stooping down to where she stands, I cup her round face in my hands. Her expression softens. "You're right, my love," I say, feeling small and silly. "You are 100 percent right."

Counting Blessings

"And you oughta tell God you're sorry for being so upset," she says emphatically, her face stern again.

I do as I am told. After all, it is November, the month for giving thanks. And, at this moment, my blessings seem measureless. Even with eggs on the ceiling.

"Give thanks unto the Lord, for he is good."
(Psalm 107:1, KJV)

Dear Lord, Your blessings are abundant. Forgive me when I complain.

Forgiveness is fragrance a violet sheds on the heels that crush it.
Anonymous

Goodbye to Love and Hate

It was raining the evening Jackie Taylor* came home and found her husband, Wade, sitting on the couch in the dark. His fortieth birthday was the next week, and Jackie had just gone out and purchased a set of golf clubs he'd been wanting for two years.

"Did you forget to pay the light bill?" Jackie teased, switching on the lamp. That's when she realized something was very wrong. Wade had a most peculiar look on his face; she had never seen that look before. "Are you OK, sweetheart? You look funny." She sat down beside him and put her hand on his shoulder.

Abruptly, Wade stood up and whirled around to face her. "It will never be easy to say this, Jackie," he sputtered, "so I'll just say it. I'm leaving you."

The room spun furiously as Jackie attempted to make sense of what she had heard. But she couldn't. Faintly, she said, "Say that again?"

Goodbye to Love and Hate

He did. "Yes. I am. I'm leaving you."

Silence surrounded them, hard and stony, like a brick wall. Finally, Jackie spoke. "After nineteen years," she said flatly. "How long have you known about this?" She tried to steady her trembling voice.

"I don't know," he said. "It's hard to explain. I didn't just wake up one morning and decide to do this."

The sounds of their two teenage daughters laughing in the bathroom filtered through the walls. "Did you know this morning? Why didn't you say something while the girls were at volleyball practice? Why tell me now when I have nothing but the night in front of me?" She was sobbing.

Wade dropped to his knees and tried to hold her.

She pushed him away angrily. "Don't," she warned. "Don't touch me, Wade. Just please get away from me."

Two weeks later, Jackie discovered the truth. Wade had left her to be with one of the instructors at the health club where he worked out, a girl six years older than his youngest daughter.

Jackie's anger came in merciless, unpredictable waves. One minute, she sobbed like a wounded child; the next, she hissed like a poisonous snake. After nineteen years of loving one man, she had been dumped like a bag of stinky trash. She vowed she would never—ever—forgive Wade.

The sleepless nights and tormented days that followed carried Jackie to the depths of despair. She ceased to live, and merely existed. She could not eat; her stomach stayed in spasms.

WHISPERS FROM HEAVEN

Church was something she stumbled to and through. Her prayers never reached the ceiling. Even though her daughters' presence in the house brought a certain amount of comfort, Jackie's pain never left. The thought of death entered her mind.

One evening, a few days before Easter, Jackie strolled down the aisles of the corner grocery store, picking up a few things for the holiday. It had been a year since her divorce. A lonely, bitter year.

As she approached the checkout lanes, she saw Wade, three lanes over, slumped across a shopping cart. He looked tired and worried. Without meaning to, Jackie felt sorry for him. At first, she considered it a knee-jerk reaction, but the more she studied him, she realized something else was happening. Standing there in the middle of the grocery store, Jackie Taylor forgave her husband. Totally and completely.

She recalls the feeling. "I can't explain what happened, but as I watched him, I just decided to forgive him. I've asked myself why dozens of times since then, and all I know is it had to be God. Because the minute I forgave him, I started to feel myself climbing out of a deep, dark pit. It was such a powerful feeling, I really thought I might faint right there in the store. I started smiling, something I hadn't done in a year, and then I started crying. It was incredible. I felt so free."

As Jackie left the store, she smelled a powerful, sweet odor and looked around. There, just outside the door, sat dozens of snow-white Easter lilies. "I had almost forgotten it was Easter," she says. "Suddenly, I remembered Jesus hanging on the cross, betrayed by loved ones, His hurt exposed, and I heard Him saying, "Father, forgive them . . ."

It was the first time Jackie had ever bought an Easter lily, but she buys one every year now. She feels kin to them. Jackie firmly believes that vowing to never forgive her husband was the cause of her emotional and physical problems. They ended the night she forgave Wade. "I thought I'd hurt Wade by never forgiving him," she says. "Instead, I nearly killed myself. Forgiving him saved my life."

"If you hold anything against anyone, forgive him, so that
your Father in heaven may forgive you your sins."
(Mark 11:25, NIV)

Father, give us the courage to forgive, so we can live again.

*Names have been changed.

Each day I learn more than I teach.
Virginia Church, *A Learner*

Simple Lessons

When Anna was three, one of her favorite pastimes was playing "church." Playing church normally meant she'd line up her baby dolls on the little bench in the foyer of the house, take her large Bible storybook, and sit in front of them. She was the teacher; they were the kids in her class at church. For hours she'd play a children's tape in her tape player while she shuffled the dolls to and from "church."

Sometimes Anna would engage her dolls in a question-and-answer session, much like the ones she and I often had. "Who was born at Christmas?" she'd ask the silent group.

"Jesus!" she'd yell out in a peculiar voice.

"Who died on a cross so you could go to heaven?" She was the teacher again.

"Jesus!" she'd yell again.

One morning, I sat at the breakfast table watching her putter around with her cornflakes. It was time for a question-and-answer session of our own. I decided on a difficult question, just to see how much she was retaining.

"Who found a silver cup in his sack of corn?" I queried.

"Noah!" she shouted, sending a spray of cornflakes and milk across the red-checkered tablecloth.

Great. "No," I told her gently. "Remember? It was the baby brother of Joseph."

She wrinkled her nose and thought a while. "I give up," she said.

"Benjamin," I said. "Remember Benjamin?"

"Mama," she said, "That's too hard for a little girl like me."

Maybe she was right. Maybe I expected too much of her.

Later in the day, she wanted me to play church with her. This particular version differed from when she played with the dolls; it required my active participation. For reasons known only to her, I needed to be the preacher. And as is the case sometimes with small congregations, I was also the song leader, the pianist, and one of the church soloists.

This day, I had just rendered a humdrum rendition of "Deep and Wide" when Anna said, "OK, Mama, now you get in the microphone and say, 'Anna Shockley, please come up.'"

So I took the microphone—an overripe banana—and said, "Anna Shockley, please come up."

She marched sternly to the piano where I sat. In my best pretend voice I said, "Mrs. Shockley, what are you going to sing for us tonight?"

"You are my helper," she said.

"OK," I said, agreeably. "I'll be your helper."

"No, Mama," she said. "That's what I'm singing, 'You Are My Helper.' "

"Hmmm." I looked thoughtful. "I don't believe I know that one. Can you play it?"

She nodded, so I slid off the piano bench. Looking earnest, she climbed on, and soon the ivories were making a joyful— OK, loud—noise unto the Lord. Her small voice lifted and fell sporadically as she sang out in a most unstructured fashion.

"You are my helper." *Clang! Bang!* "You are my helper." *Clang! Bang!* "You are my helper when somebody needs a helper." *Clang! Bang! Clang! Bang!* "When I need a song, you are my helper." *Clang! Bang!* "When I'm on my knees, you are my helper." *Clang! Bang!*

With her eyes clamped shut, she belted out about three rounds of this. At last, she sat smiling and breathless. "OK, ma'am," she said, turning to me. "It's your turn now." I hesitated briefly. "No," she said abruptly. "Church is over."

I let out a great sigh of relief, for I feared I could never follow such a moving act. Besides, a giant lump had mysteriously settled in my throat.

Without question, her song to God had been heartfelt. I remembered all the times I had offered the Lord petty lip service, my mind on frivolous concerns. Hearing my daughter deliver such a genuine praise offering opened a window inside of me, forcing me to examine my soul's staleness. *Where on earth had she come up with that song?* I wondered.

As I prepared the evening meal, I glanced at the artwork she'd brought home from church and stuck on the refrigerator the week before. Every week the teacher made each pupil a little memento with a Bible verse written on it, hoping to help the little ones remember the day's lesson. This one was a piece of red construction paper in the shape of Anna's left hand. In the middle of the small palm were printed these words: *I will help thee. Isaiah 41:10.*

Staring at those four simple words, I smiled. Now I knew where Anna's song had come from. My daughter was learning. And in the process, so was I.

"From the lips of children and infants you have ordained praise."
(Matthew 21:16, NIV)

Lord, when my worship becomes stiff and formal, You send a child to point the way.

Cherish all your happy moments. They will make a fine cushion for old age.
Booth Tarkington

The Day of My Conversion

As I put away breakfast dishes one sunny morning, my sister phoned and asked me to come help her clean out some closets, to dispose of some things. For twenty years, she had thrown out remarkably little. After vain attempts to cure her, I had finally come to accept her for what she was: a pack rat. Now, she was asking me to wade through old photographs, cards, letters, souvenirs of her former self. The unbelievable had happened!

Confident I would see she kept no more than necessary, I quickly accepted her offer, before she could change her mind.

Cheerfully, I drove to her home, rang the doorbell, let myself in, and strolled to the back bedroom. There she stood, surrounded by a heap of cardboard boxes.

"Just getting started," she said heartily, reaching for another box in the dim closet.

Surprised by her enthusiasm, I eagerly accepted the bulky carton she handed down from the top shelf, carried it to the

The Day of My Conversion

bed, and dutifully opened it.

"No, no," she said, waving her hands. "Don't open them; I'm just going to trash everything."

"*Everything?*"

"Yeah."

"Without even *looking* at it?" My voice had a peculiar ring.

"Yeah," she explained. "If I haven't looked at it in this many years, why bother now?" She laughed.

I said nothing but wondered what had come over her.

And then—unable to stop myself—I peeked inside the large brown box in front of me.

A mistake.

"You're not throwing *this* away!" I gasped, pulling out a small cardboard plaque.

"Why?" she said, not looking. "What is it?"

"What *is* it?" I said, much louder than necessary. "It's Humpty-Dumpty-Sat-On-A-Wall. That's what it is!"

She cast me a look.

"Do you have any idea how *old* this thing is?" I asked, sounding so quivery I sat down. "This—this is priceless!" So extreme was my statement, I hesitated, to be sure I had heard myself correctly.

Silently, I stared at the colorful picture of Humpty Dumpty straddling a tall brick wall, all the king's horses and all the king's men looking up from below, pale and panicked.

Then I spied a tiny, rusty circle at the top of the plaque and recalled the countless nights I fell asleep with this little plaque thumbtacked above my bed, my sister sleeping beside me.

I felt an odd stirring in my chest. Something akin to yearning. Something I dared not try to unravel.

A lump settled, unexpectedly, in my throat. I looked at my sister. But she was reaching for another box, unaware of my inner struggle.

Cradling Humpty Dumpty in one arm, I dug deeper into the open carton. Here was the miniature cedar chest—a souvenir from Alabama—I used to pack with shiny buttons and polished stones, pretending they were costly jewels from a boyfriend. Carefully, I lifted the tiny lid and stuck my nose inside. The remembered scent of cedar had long since vanished, but suddenly the little chest seemed like a childhood friend, one who kept my secrets and shared my dreams.

From all appearances, the boxes before me were stuffed with similar objects. If I let my sister throw all these things away, I could never again recapture this feeling. I felt downright weepy.

Placing the chest aside, I turned to my sister. "Look," I said firmly, "I don't think you should just throw all this stuff away."

She laughed.

"You could at least have a garage sale. Something!"

She laughed again.

I knew she was laughing at me. For years, I'd been the one hassling her about saving things; about not being able to separate the past from the present. If you don't use it, I preached, sell it. Trash it. Clear the clutter. She had finally come to her senses. So what had come over me?

Appearing thoughtful, she said, "Just lay the things you might want over to the side. When we're done, you can take them with you. Or whatever . . ."

Surveying the relics before me, I almost wept with relief.

The rest of the afternoon moved smoothly. For every item my sister tossed, I found one to keep. Her closet was so empty it echoed. My pile, however, rose dangerously high, yet I couldn't part with a single thing.

When at last it came time to go, I could not believe my eyes. Boxes lined the trunk of my little car. Meekly, I waved goodbye and drove out of sight, the rear of the car sagging.

On the drive home, I was totally converted. I began seeing my relics as a person might view her life—the events they represented, whether wonderful or painful, created the person I had become. The contents of those boxes were pieces of history; to destroy them would be to destroy a part of myself. For like bleached shells scattered aimlessly along the sandy shores, vacant, stony houses of nothing, so are we without our memories; without our treasures of yesterday.

"Rejoice . . . in thy youth."
(Ecclesiastes 11:9, KJV)

Dear Jesus, thank You for the joys of yesterday. May they become a springboard into tomorrow.

Children need love, especially when they do not deserve it.
H. S. Hulbert

Finding the Good

erry was a quiet child, aloof and somewhat clownish. Every weekend, without fail, he wandered aimlessly into the little primary class, where a handful of youngsters gathered.

Plopping into his chair, Jerry would let out a dramatic yawn—with as much gusto as is possible for an eight-year-old to muster. Then, looking terribly bored, he would frame his small face in his hands, wrinkle his square forehead, and stare blankly at the ceiling.

No amount of coaxing from the teacher succeeded in obtaining Jerry's cooperation; he appeared perfectly content at being her "thorn in the flesh."

When storytime began, Jerry—as if on cue—would mysteriously unwind from his daydreaming posture and don a small cloak of childish wit. This generally produced a euphoric reaction among his fellow primaries.

Close to tears, the teacher patiently would try to bring the

Finding the Good

little group to order, but how could she possibly compete with such antics as snickering, snorting, and belching—which Jerry so often rendered? Finally, at wit's end, the frustrated teacher resigned.

That's when my mother became Jerry's teacher, but not before she was cautioned aplenty by the former teacher: "You're going to have a lot of trouble with Jerry; he's so unruly."

Although she keeps it well disguised, my mother is a bit stubborn herself—my two sisters will back me up on this. Time would tell whether or not she could manage Jerry.

With much prudence, Mother quietly observed for the first few weeks, carefully planning her strategy. Finally, the day arrived; it was time to see if Jerry was salvageable.

The little tykes rambled nonchalantly into the tiny classroom and noisily took their seats. A brooding Jerry brought up the rear, looking irritated, naturally. After seating himself abruptly, he let out his infamous yawn, followed by a thunderous belch.

Contemplatively, Mother busied herself as the youngsters settled in. Then she stood—activity sheets in hand—and said, "Jerry, would you pass out the activity sheets today?" She flashed a disarming smile.

The stunned Jerry took the papers from her and, with the hint of a smile on his face, distributed them to the class.

From that day forward, Jerry blossomed. He displayed the genuine interest in the class, even joining in during the group discussions at the close of each lesson. At times, he even *offered* his assistance to the teacher, handing out papers or moving chairs.

When asked how she did it, Mother said it appeared Jerry needed to be appreciated, to be needed. Instead of constantly telling him what *not* to do—don't talk, don't slouch, don't interrupt—she told him something *to* do.

As simple as this may sound, it holds a ton of truth. No matter how ill behaved, every child possesses a redeeming quality. Search diligently for it. And when you find it—regardless of how insignificant it may seem—nurture it with the greatest of care.

> *"Inasmuch as ye have done it unto one of the least of these . . . , ye have done it unto me."*
> (Matthew 25:40, KJV)

Who can we lead today, Lord?

*It is in the enjoyment and not in mere possession that makes
for happiness.*
Michel DeMontaigne

Just What
I Needed

When my husband and I married, we lived in a two-bedroom trailer in the back of a trailer park. While the trailer was attractive, I wasn't so sure I wanted it for my home.

The lot flooded when it rained, the scrawny tree in the front yard looked like an overgrown weed, and the furniture didn't match anything. The trailer just wasn't me. Especially the gold velour chair. To make matters worse, my husband worked long hours, leaving me with ample time for brooding.

One rainy afternoon, I slumped in the wobbly gold chair and longed for the big old rocker I'd spent hours in at my parents' house. I missed Mama's homemade biscuits and the lace-edged hand towels she left in the bathrooms. *That* was a home.

"Lord," I prayed, "please help Stan and me find a real home." It would take a miracle.

I got up from the chair and trudged to the mailbox, wishing

for a letter from home. Hopeful, I turned the key in the box. All that tumbled out was a light bill.

Disheartened, I turned to go back and noticed a thin, elderly woman coming, her head bent under a black umbrella. When she waved, I recognized her; she lived next door.

"Haven't heard from my son in a while," she said, fishing in her pocket for her key.

Not having the heart to walk away, I sidled up beside her and waited.

"Yoo-hoo! Lookee here." The old woman pulled out a crinkled envelope and kissed it.

As we headed home, I said, "My name is Dayle. I live in the trailer next to you."

She squinted at me from under her umbrella. "OK," she said slowly, as if a mystery had just unfolded. "I'm Mrs. Baxter."

Even though our friendship consisted of little more than an occasional wave and a "Howdy!" across the lawn, I felt less alone when Stan worked, knowing Mrs. Baxter was there.

One afternoon I realized I hadn't seen her in several days, so I walked over, knocked on the door, and was relieved when she opened it. She looked surprised to see me. "I was just checking on you," I explained.

"Yeah," she said loudly. "Come on in."

For a while, I sat on the faded blue couch while she shuffled around in the kitchen, making small talk. She was an eccentric mixture of youth and age. I soon learned her favorite snack was

Just What I Needed

a garlic and butter sandwich, her son lived in San Antonio, and she had been a widow longer than she could remember.

Her living-room walls were smothered with photographs in cheap frames. I stood to get a closer look. They all had one thing in common: a little boy who soon grew into a teenager, then a handsome young man. Beside him in every shot was a tall, thin woman—plainly, Mrs. Baxter.

"Is this you and your son here in all these pictures?" I asked.

She joined me. "That's my boy," she said. She sighed. "Yep, lots of memories on that there wall."

Then, giving me an odd look, Mrs. Baxter pointed a bony finger under my nose. "Don't forget to make some memories, young lady," she said, half scolding. "Today!" she barked, startling me.

An awkward silence settled in the little room. I felt young and dumb. I realized this old lady had just imparted a word of wisdom, yet I hadn't a clue as to how to respond. I simply patted her stooped shoulder and nodded.

"Thanks for coming by," she said abruptly, as if signaling the end of our visit. I said goodbye, leaving her waving at the door.

Back in the trailer, I sat in the ugly gold chair and stared at the gloomy walls. I thought about Mrs. Baxter's words: "Don't forget to make some memories, young lady." In this place? Did I dare?

The next morning I drove to the paint store, selected a few color cards, and eagerly showed them to my husband.

WHISPERS FROM HEAVEN

"What do you think about this color?" I pointed to a square of pale peach. "I think it would brighten up the room, make it look bigger. Don't you?"

"If you want to," he said, "that's fine with me."

Feeling better than I'd felt in months, I rushed to the paint store, purchased a gallon of "peach cloud" paint, two brushes, a roller, and a dropcloth.

Back home, I washed the bleak walls with soap and water, let them dry, then earnestly set out to give the room a face lift. Though the job proved long and tedious, by the next evening I sat beaming at the results. Even the gold chair possessed a freshness.

Little by little, the trailer changed. My dad helped us build a roomy redwood porch on the front; I painted the bedrooms; we installed fresh carpets on the floor and fashionable curtains at the windows.

Six years later, after our daughter was born, we sold the trailer and purchased a home. The day before the new owners were having the trailer moved, I asked Stan to drive by. As we rounded the curve, I saw the redwood porch pulled away from the front door, the skirting scattered on the ground. I was unprepared for my reaction.

Seeing the trailer being uprooted sent a surprise ache to my heart. I realized a part of me still drifted through its empty rooms. Behind those doors, I had experienced life's pleasures and pains. A flood of memories filled me.

Just What I Needed

Clearly, the trailer wasn't the only thing that had changed. I had changed too. For without question, this trailer I once found so undesirable had—through the years—become my cherished home, a sanctuary of sorts.

Wistfully, I glanced at the lot where Mrs. Baxter's trailer used to sit. I recalled those early depressing days when I had asked God for a new place to live.

Instead, He had sent me to check on an old woman one afternoon. A woman who helped me discover that we shouldn't waste a perfectly good today while waiting on tomorrow's miracle.*

"I have learned to be content whatever the circumstances."
(Philippians 4:11, NIV)

Lord, remind me that the time to be happy is now.

* A version of some of the material included in this chapter appeared in *Guideposts* magazine and is reprinted by permission. Copyright © 1994 by Guideposts Associates, Inc, Carmel, NY 10512.

Happiness taken for granted will slowly but surely perish.
Perry Tanksley

Hidden Treasures

wo weeks before Easter, I stood staring at the clothes in my closet. "I am so sick of these old clothes," I growled to my husband. "I haven't had a new dress in two years."

"Well, don't go getting any wild ideas," Stan said sharply. "You know we can't afford it right now."

"But it's Easter," I pleaded. "I'll find something on sale."

"Dayle, we just can't afford it, so forget it." The way he said it, so matter of factly, angered me. I stomped from the room to lick my wounds.

In my heart, I knew my husband was right. Three years earlier, I had chosen to give up my job and stay at home after my daughter's birth. Even though the joys of full-time mothering surpassed my expectations, I did miss the luxuries an extra income brought: new clothes, new shoes, an occasional night on the town.

The next morning, I stood at the front door and waved my

husband off to work. For a while, I admired the delicate blooms on the crab-apple tree in the front yard. But then, my eye caught a glimpse of the weeds spilling out of terribly neglected flower beds.

As I contemplated such trials of home ownership, my neighbor across the street—much to my chagrin—appeared around the corner, spade and shears in hand.

For a while, I watched Amy's small form hunched over a couple of rosebushes, a pleasant look on her face. She and her husband were retired, so they could often be seen puttering around the yard at odd hours of the day.

As a mother of a three-year-old, I envied their seemingly carefree existence. Even though I found motherhood exhilarating, it sometimes left me drained. To prove my point, my daughter chose that exact moment to dump an entire box of animal crackers on the living-room floor.

It must be wonderful, I thought, *to have nothing to do but pamper rosebushes all morning.* Just then, Amy glanced up, saw me at the door, and waved in my direction.

So inviting was her wave that I scooped up my daughter, ignored the crackers, and headed to the garage. Collecting my gardening gloves and a rusty trowel, I marched relentlessly down the driveway. Feeling like a reckless barber, I plopped on the ground, determined to give the beds a much-needed shaving.

What appeared to be an easy task soon found me short of breath. This was our first spring as homeowners, and these beds had obviously not been cultivated in a while. The roots of the overgrowth went deep. To make matters worse, for every weed I plucked out, Anna found one to chew on.

After an exhausting hour of digging and pulling, I was just about to call it quits. Then the trowel struck a hard object in the ground, producing a clinking sound, like metal striking metal. With one hand, I carefully groped beneath the soil and gasped when I pulled out a man's gold signet ring. Thrilled with my find, I wondered whom it belonged to and what I should do with it.

Later that evening, I decided to phone Michelle and Paul, the previous owners of the home. When I told Michelle what I had found, she was amazed—and thrilled. It seemed that Paul had lost this ring several years ago; they thought he misplaced it at the mall. Even though she said the ring had little monetary worth, it was a gift from his mother and held great sentimental value for her husband. My discovery seemed like a dream come true.

After Michelle made arrangements to pick up the ring, I sat on the couch for a long while, just thinking about the odds of anyone ever having found it. The knowledge that I had been the one to uncover this hidden treasure, after so long a time, filled me with a unique satisfaction.

That evening, after giving Anna her bath, I watched while she and her father engaged in their nightly game of chase. Dressed in silky pink pajamas, her rich chestnut hair held back by two yellow barrettes, Anna raced into the room squealing, her father fast on her heels. "Betcha can't catch me, Daddy," she said, her breath coming out in great gulps, her eyes sparkling, anticipating the chase.

As I sat there, something awakened in me. In a sense, I uncovered my own hidden treasures that night. Treasures finer than new suits of clothes, more precious than gold signet rings. How could I have been so blind? Priceless possessions lay in giggly piles on the living-room floor.

"The Lord shall open unto thee his good treasure."
(Deuteronomy 28:12, KJV)

Help me, Lord, to see that my most valuable treasures are often the ones I take for granted.

Love is the reward of Love.
Schiller

Discoveries

I never would have believed that I would be standing inside a doll hospital, contemplating a new $75 body for my little daughter's doll. *Just buy another doll,* I should tell myself. But here I am, clutching the frazzled doll in my arms, listening to what the young man—dressed as a real doctor—says.

"We would have to fit her with a totally new body," he says, reaching behind him to where one sits in a bin. "Like this." He holds out a headless body, then takes the doll I have brought.

"This little doll has simply been loved to death," he says. "She has," he adds, as if to convince me. Gingerly, he fingers one arm that now hangs by a few thin threads and flashes me a gloomy smile.

I turn away to hide my sudden emotions. A childhood gift to me from my father, the doll is, clearly, exhausted. It's hard to believe the doll was in perfect condition when I gave her to my daughter. Now, a body once firm and stout is soiled, limp as a

Discoveries

dishrag. Except for that unruly cowlick on top, most of her hair has fallen out. Her frumpy appearance has wounded my pride on many occasions. That is why I am here.

"What about her hair?" I ask the doctor. "Can you do anything with it?"

He touches the pale hair—what's left of it—and clucks his tongue. "I'm afraid the hair is hopeless," he says. "But—we *could* put a wig on her." He seems thrilled.

"*A wig!*"

Reaching under the counter, the doctor pulls out a small cardboard box and opens it. A dozen wads of hair tumble out, scattering around us like a group of frightened hamsters. He selects a lustrous blond one, holds up the doll a bit and, unceremoniously, plops it onto her tiny head.

"Now, this wig would totally change the little doll's appearance."

An understatement. I fight back giggles.

"It would sort of give her a whole new—a different personality," he offers.

To say the least. "That's just not Sunshine," I say, frowning at the mop of golden curls perched haphazardly atop her small head. She looks ridiculous.

"No?"

"No." I slump over the counter, overwhelmed with the moment. "I had no idea this would turn into a major ordeal! My goodness—she's just a *doll.*"

WHISPERS FROM HEAVEN

"Not just a doll," the young man reminds me. "But one that has been loved for a very long time."

A decision eludes me at the moment. Abruptly, I say goodbye-I'll-think-about-it and leave the "doctor" amid his headless bodies and synthetic curls.

I stumble to my car, crawl in, and methodically turn onto the main street.

Sunshine lies quietly beside me. I am unsure what to do with her. I need wisdom. "Oh, Lord," I whisper, hardly believing I am praying about a spent doll, "please help me know what to do with Sunshine."

The next morning I am cleaning out Anna's closet. Anna stands placidly beside me, Sunshine dangling across one arm. "Why don't you play with Cecille?" I casually suggest, thrusting a pretty brown-eyed Cabbage Patch doll toward her. "See, Anna, this baby has big brown eyes like yours," I coax.

Nothing doing. Protectively, like a lion defending a cub, Anna's arm tightens around Sunshine's droopy body. She gives me a stern stare. "But I *love* Sunshine, Mommy," she explains, her voice fearless. "Her's my *baby*." Sensing defeat, I sigh long and hard but say nothing as this three-year-old mother scuttles off down the hall, baby in tow.

In the afternoon, Anna and I ride across town to check out a sale at a ritzy ladies' boutique. Sunshine sits prominently between us, appearing rather pathetic in her soiled blue dress.

"Let's not take your baby in, Anna," I say as we pull into the

crowded parking lot.

"Why, Mommy?" She is puzzled.

"Just this once, Anna. Please. We'll be right back."

"But, Mommy, *why?*" she presses.

And then, out it gushes, like an erupting volcano. "Because she is just too ugly! That's why!" The minute the cruel words hurl out, I ache to recall them.

There is a heavy silence, during which I long for death. Speechless, I watch Anna stare down at her most prized possession, confusion sweeping across her cherubic face. I can tell she has never considered such a thing.

In a flash she lifts Sunshine from the seat, crushes her firmly to her chest, and announces—in no uncertain terms, "Her is not ugee, Mommy. Not to me!"

I feel as if my repentant heart will explode. Of course, Anna is right. She *loves* the doll; nothing else matters.

That's just the way you see me, Lord, I think. *Just as my daughter sees beauty in this ragged doll, Your love for me is not swayed by my physical appearance. Whether I'm rich or poor, fat or skinny, it doesn't matter. Never mind that I can't afford the finest clothes or contribute the largest offerings. You accept me—and want me!— just as I am.* This discovery moves me.

"I'm sorry, Anna," I say meekly, taking the doll. "Sunshine is not ugly. In fact, she looks very, very pretty. Please forgive me. I don't know what I was thinking about."

Anna nods her head and smiles, relieved.

I hand her the doll. "And, yes, you may take her into the store."

Hand in hand we stroll through the warm sunshine, each grateful for the power of grace.

"Though your sins be as scarlet, they shall be as white as snow."
(Isaiah 1:18, KJV)

Lord, through Your eyes, we are beautiful.

A mother is a mother still, the holiest thing alive.
Samuel Taylor Coleridge

Adjustments

onday morning, 6:30. It is the kind of August morning that promises showers. I am tiptoeing through the kitchen like a burglar, carrying a basket brimming with dirty laundry. My two-month-old daughter sleeps peacefully in the other end of the house. Her early feeding done, I am determined to get a head start on the day—something I haven't done since bringing her home from the hospital. Besides, it's been a week since I opened the clothes hamper; things are getting a bit smelly.

Being a mother satisfies me, but until my daughter's birth, I never knew the true meaning of the word *tired*. The days creep into the nights, leaving me weary with fatigue, wondering if I will live to see her start school.

With heavy hands, I load the washing machine, sneak into the kitchen, and turn the burner on under the kettle. In the darkness, I sit waiting for the water to warm. I am exhausted. The living room resembles a garage sale; it's been weeks since I looked at a newspaper, listened to the news, heard my favorite song. My world revolves around a plump little girl named Anna who makes great smacking noises and smells of baby powder and cotton gowns.

As I gulp down the last swallow of coffee, I have one wish: three hours of uninterrupted sleep. But just as I set the cup on the table, Anna is awake again.

Holding her close, I suddenly become selfish. *When am I ever going to rest? Or get the house cleaned? Or cook a decent meal?* I wonder, surprised by my own anger. *Motherhood is a constant demand of my time, Lord,* I say to myself more than to anyone else. *I'm a person too! I need things too! Like rest . . . and sleep . . . and a big shoulder!* I feel like crying.

And then, as gently as the summer shower splattering the windowpane outside, the Lord speaks to me. Not audibly, but quietly He seems to say to me: *A soul is worth more than the whole world. Don't you know that? I've given you this little soul. Please look after her for Me. Nurture her. Care for her. Teach her.*

At once, I marvel. Slumped in the folds of the rocking chair, I see the beauty of myself. God did not see me as an exhausted body in a baggy housecoat but as the keeper of a soul. This revelation soothes me, refreshes me.

I look down into the face of my precious baby. From some-where deep inside, I feel a stirring, an intense longing to be God's greatest baby sitter. Wholeheartedly, unreservedly, I embrace this hallowed assignment called motherhood.

Adjustments

"Have mercy upon me, O Lord; for I am weak."
(Psalm 6:2, KJV)

Dear Lord, life is full of adjustments, but none so important as the adjustments of motherhood. Be my guide as I sail these unfamiliar waters.

The world, when seen through a little child's eyes, greatly resembles paradise.
Anonymous

The Bargain

At 10:30 Tuesday morning, my doorbell rang. I stepped to the door, glanced out, and opened it. There on the porch stood a thin, tow-headed little boy, about seven or eight years old, I guessed. His eyes appeared large behind the thick black-rimmed glasses covering his narrow face. In his hands, he tightly clutched a small brown paper bag.

"Yes?" I said, my lack of enthusiasm obvious. I did detest peddlers—even young ones.

"Hello, ma'am," he began, a shade of nervousness in his small voice. "Uh . . ." He glanced down toward the bag, cleared his throat, then hurriedly stated his mission. "Would you care to buy a surprise?" He seemed skeptical.

In my lifetime, I had been asked to buy dozens of things, but a surprise had never been one of them. Totally taken aback, I found myself speechless. My imagination ran rampant as I attempted to interpret his unusual offer: *Was it a leftover lunch? A*

The Bargain

dead frog? Ugh! I shuddered at the thought.

"A surprise?" My voice came out at least two octaves higher than it normally did.

His face registering hope, the lad dropped to his knees and abruptly spilled the contents of the little bag onto the front porch. A long pause, during which I stared down at an array of colors and shapes, still uncertain what was before me.

On closer inspection, I saw he had made small envelopes out of different colors of construction paper. On the outside of each one, he had pasted odd-shaped pieces of nothing. A tab, of sorts, was folded over the envelope and sealed with a sticker.

Apparently, he *had* gone to a great deal of trouble—If he created them all—but they seemed rather foolish to me. I opened my mouth to decline, when I stopped short. Bits and pieces of a Scripture passed before me. Something about doing it unto the "least of these." Eyeing his birdlike arms, the description fit.

So instead of saying No, I said, "What's in them?"

His head sprang up, causing his heavy glasses to take a sudden plunge on his little freckled nose. Quickly, he adjusted them and stood up, looking awfully earnest. "Well, it's like this, ma'am," he explained, fetching one of the crudely made envelopes. "If you buy one of these here envelopes, there's two surprise stickers inside." He punched the word *stickers* as if it would capture my undivided attention.

The world grew quiet as I stared intently at the envelopes. And then back at the little boy. Big blue eyes looked long and hard into mine. How could I turn him away? What could it possibly hurt?

"How much are they?" I asked.

"Oh . . ." his voice drifted off in the wind. "A dime?"

It was a definite question.

Unwilling to argue, I went in search of my wallet.

A look of satisfaction brushed his freckled face as I placed the thin dime into his small hand. He handed me a dark blue envelope, quickly gathered his wares, and mumbled a hurried thank-you. Puckering his lips into a whistle, he skipped down the driveway and out of sight.

Strangely, I felt relieved as I turned slowly into the house and locked the door. Carefully, I opened my purchase.

Peering out at me from their hiding places were two yellow smiley-face stickers. Without thinking, I smiled back. *A smile never hurt anybody,* I thought, sticking them on the refrigerator.

No doubt, the lad has long since spent the dime I gave him, but I've kept his "surprise" on my refrigerator door. Not only does it remind me to smile, it also reminds me that I must give something away in order to get something back.

"Who hath despised the day of small things?"
(Zechariah 4:10, KJV)

Jesus, Your best surprises often come in little packages.

There are no hopeless situations; there are only men who have grown hopeless about them.
Clare Booth Luce

Possibilities

ne evening, I sat in church listening to my pastor talk about God's ability to do anything. Raised in a minister's home, this message was not a new one to me. But no longer a child, I found myself . . . yes, doubting. It wasn't that God had ever failed me; He hadn't. Nor was it that God had never healed my body; He had. I *knew* He could do anything.

Maybe it was just that the struggles facing me this night loomed larger than life itself. Because I thought my trials too deep and too dark to share with fellow Christians, I found myself bent over from the heavy load.

Often, I tried to convince myself that I deserved to suffer. After all, I had been the one who refused counsel, plunging headlong into this destructive situation. Maybe this—the mental anguish, the hopelessness, the feeling of failure—was the penalty I must pay for such foolish choices.

"God wants to take your negatives and turn them into positives," the preacher was saying. "Remember," he said, "a car's battery has a negative and a positive connection. You hold the negative; God holds the positive. Put them together, and anything is possible."

That evening I crawled into bed thinking about those words but unable to shake my remorse. Feeling like a total flop, I pulled the covers close and breathed a solitary prayer: *Lord, please make something good out of this mess I've made.*

The next morning I stood at my bay window, staring out across the backyard. Except for a dozen scattered shrubs, which managed to survive the winter's freezing temperatures, the yard appeared completely void of color. Trees stood naked, not a leaf in sight. Grass that once caressed bare feet rested brown and strawlike. The yard's barrenness seemed to mirror my soul.

In an effort to cheer myself, I bundled up and drove to a local antique mall. As I strolled through the aisles, my eye caught a large mural painted on the back wall. For a while, I stood admiring the white stone fence surrounding a glorious array of flowers—zinnias, peonies, snapdragons, marigolds—exploding above the lush jade grass. In the center, under an azure sky, a narrow pebble path led to a stately gazebo. Breathtaking!

Just then, the mural moved. Astonished, I realized I had been staring at the back of two garage doors opening out to the loading dock.

My heart leapt. I knew, beyond a doubt, God had brought me to this place to be encouraged. If a garage door could become a work of art, surely the Creator could transform my mistakes into a masterpiece.

"All things are possible to him that believeth."
(Mark 9:23, KJV)

Thank You, Father, for Your ability to turn our blunders into beauty.

55

Great works are performed not by strength but by perseverance.
Samuel Johnson

Planting and Reaping

You could never call Faith Williams a quitter. In a day when the average American moves fourteen times over a lifetime, Faith has lived in the same house for forty years. Statistics reveal that one in two marriages will end in divorce; Faith and her husband, James, were married forty-nine years, separated by his death in 1983.

Not long ago, Faith gave her fiftieth piano recital. And while some folks hop from church to church, seeking the ultimate something or other, Faith has attended the same church since its founding in 1927. For more than sixty years, she has taught in the children's department.

But now, she was considering—of all things—resigning her position. Almost eighty years old, she figured a younger person could take her place, ushering in fresh ideas, new concepts. Maybe it was time to move over.

For several weeks, Faith pondered this weighty decision, asking the Lord for wisdom. Teaching the children was, as she put it, her "life." She did not want to make a choice and live to regret it.

On Friday, Faith strolled out to the garden she has plowed, tilled, and planted every year—alone—since her husband's death. When she came to the three hills of cucumbers, she reached down and picked about two quarts of tiny ones. Seeing none left and no more blooms on the vines, Faith decided the cucumbers were done for the year. She had already canned all she wanted, with plenty left over to give away to friends.

The following Tuesday morning, Faith visited the garden again, this time to see if any tomatoes were ripe enough to harvest. That's when something else caught her attention: the cucumber vines. In utter disbelief, Faith stared at the vines. They were loaded down with cucumbers! Some as long as the distance between her wrist and elbow and almost as big around as her arm!

That's impossible, she thought, blinking her eyes. *It simply cannot be happening. Those vines were empty last Friday.* Still, cucumbers hung all over the vines; she harvested almost a bushel.

Standing in the kitchen, staring down at the cucumbers spilling out of the double sink, Faith realized she was beholding a miracle. *But why?* she wondered. *I don't need any more cucumbers, Lord. Why did You allow this to happen?*

For a while, she toyed with a few ideas as to why such a miraculous thing would happen. Surely, there had to be a reason.

And then, she knew the answer. Like a gentle summer breeze, it seemed the Lord said, *Faith, you thought you were through with those cucumber vines. Neither am I through with you. If you stay faithful to your calling, you can bear fruit like this, even in your old age.*

Rejoicing at God's mindfulness, Faith not only didn't resign her position at the church, she took on several new piano students as well. "I am filled with a fresh inspiration and desire," she says. "God knew I would be perfectly miserable if I had quit the work I love so much."

Imagine the bountiful harvest after sixty years of planting.

"Whatever your hand finds to do, do it with all your might."
(Ecclesiastes 9:10, NIV)

Lord, You see no difference in the young and the old; only the willingness of the heart.

Be still, sad heart! and cease repining. Behind the clouds is the sun still shining.
Longfellow, *The Rainy Day*

A Hole in My Heart

It was the final days of frivolity, perhaps. Texas fields exploded with bluebonnets under a dazzling sun. I had met and fallen head over heels in love with James, a charmer with eyes the color of a robin's egg. By spring's end, we were planning a late-summer wedding.

In retrospect, I should have known the relationship could not endure. For while we pledged to love each other, we didn't *like* each other. My habits annoyed him; his annoyed me. But still, like a mule wearing blinders, I plunged full-speed ahead, oblivious to the nagging doubts in my mind.

The ensuing days rocked with activity. There were friends to contact, photographers to hire, invitations to order, bakeries to visit, and, of course, a wedding gown to buy.

Late one evening, three weeks before the wedding date, my sister and I addressed the final invitation. We counted them: four hundred exactly. "I'll buy stamps tomorrow," I told her.

WHISPERS FROM HEAVEN

"Let's go to bed."

As I fell in bed, the phone rang. It was James calling to tell me the wedding was off. Just like that. Even though he offered explanations, nothing made sense to me. My world had just fallen in pieces around me. Nothing he said could fill the hole left in my heart.

For two days, I lay on the floor and bawled. I wanted to die. My mother came and went from my room. She said all a mother can say, but no words could soothe me. This deep sense of loss was something I'd never experienced on such a personal level. I loved James, and I could not imagine having to spend the rest of my life without him. Not only that, how would I ever face my friends again? I was humiliated and wounded beyond words. The pain of it all was agonizing. "I don't think I'll ever get over this," I told my mother. "Ever."

Three weeks later, I woke to the sound of thunder. It sounded like a call to arms. I hurried to the hall closet, pulled out an old raincoat, my mother's umbrella, and headed out the front door.

"Where are you going?" My mother's voice stopped me.

"I've got to get out of this house."

"But it's fixing to rain . . ."

"I know," I said, leaving her staring after me with a troubled face.

Outside, sooty clouds dotted the thick gray sky; they looked ready to burst. With no destination, I marched staunchly down the narrow road, as if to march away from my grief. The thunder rumbled behind me, like a big bass drum. When I reached the curve in the road, it had started to rain, slowly at first, then in great sheets. Opening the umbrella, I trudged homeward, the rain splashing in my shoes. "God," I said out loud, "please help this ache to go away."

In the house, I collapsed in a heap on the couch and stayed there several hours until a loud rap came at the door. I opened it and was surprised to see my pastor and his assistant standing there.

"May we come in, Dayle?" they asked.

As we settled in the living room, they told me why they had come. "We wanted to stop by and offer you some words of encouragement."

Did I ever need it!

In the next few minutes, these wise servants of the Lord shared themselves with me. They told me I was a person of worth; that I would find love again. They said that God doesn't always appear to make sense to us, because we are so frail in our own knowledge. But, as a child trusts her father, they assured me I could trust the Lord. And, finally, they encouraged me not to look back but move steadily ahead, allowing this experience to make me stronger instead of weaker. As they talked, I felt the hole in my heart closing up a little.

At the door, I waved as these men of God got in their car and drove away. As they disappeared from sight, I saw it had stopped raining. And then I observed a curious thing. The clouds that still hovered dark and threatening were being pushed steadily along by a relentless gust of wind from the south. It was then I knew I would survive. The rains would come, the storms would blow, but they could not last forever.

"He healeth the broken in heart, and bindeth up their wounds."
(Psalm 147:3, KJV)

When those we love leave us, Lord, thank You for sending encouragers.

Today gives us a chance to love, to work, to play, and to look up at the stars.
Henry Van Dyke

A Starry Night

I don't know if she'll be an astronaut or not, but my daughter, Anna, has always been fascinated by stars. After a recent month of rainy days and soggy nights, she delighted in discovering a star-studded sky one evening.

"Mama," she told me excitedly, "I'm gonna go in the backyard with Princess and sing "Catch a Falling Star and Put It in Your Pocket." Since I was battling a terrible headache, I agreed.

Smiling, I watched her skip out the door to her beloved collie dog and a brilliant night sky. Occasionally, I'd pass the window and catch a glimpse of her little form swaying gently in the swing, her face turned upward, Princess constant at her feet.

In a while, Anna strolled into the house, her hands cupped as if holding a precious treasure. She had been crying.

"Anna, what's the matter?"

"Mama," she said, wistfully. "Jesus has been talking to me out there."

WHISPERS FROM HEAVEN

From the look on her shining face, I didn't doubt it for one minute. "He has?" I asked, wiping a tear from the corner of her eye. "Well, what did He say?"

Still cupping her hands together, she said, "He told me that He loved me and that He died for me." She held out empty palms. "And these are all the kisses He blew down to me," she said.

Before I could find my voice, Anna tiptoed into her room and called out, "Don't look, Mama! I'm putting them in a secret place so when I feel bad I can just go get one of God's kisses."

I peeked around the corner just in time to see her bare feet sticking out from behind her bedroom door. She was hiding the kisses. "Before you hide them all," I called to her, "do you think I could have just one? My head is feeling really bad, and I think one of those kisses would make it feel much better."

In a flash, she was beside me. Tenderly, she touched my forehead with her finger. "That's from Jesus, with love," she told me. Then she kissed me. "And that's from Anna."

In that moment I knew heaven had, indeed, kissed the earth, and a little piece of starlight had landed right in my living room.

"Except ye be converted, and become as little children, ye shall not enter into the kingdom of heaven."
(Matthew 18:3, KJV)

Father, give me a child's heart.

Our Lord has written the promise of the resurrection in every leaf in springtime.
Martin Luther

Death's Colors

On a sultry day in summer, I watch my husband trudge up the steps of our home, looking grim. The past few weeks have been draining. His father, Ernest, has undergone a battery of tests after a routine checkup revealed a spot on one of his lungs. Hoping for the best, we fear the worst.

I tense as Stan opens the front door, letting in a rush of oppressive Texas heat.

"Well? What did they say?" I ask, trying to sound cheerful.

He draws his breath in sharply. "It doesn't look good."

Silence hangs between us like a black blanket.

"Daddy has between three months and two years to live. Lung cancer."

Ernest is fifty-nine.

Without speaking, Stan and I reach out to each other, our hearts one giant ache.

For several weeks, I manage to keep my spirits up. Ernest

looks good. He eats well. He still drives Mildred around town. I find myself thinking this handsome, robust man cannot possibly be terminally ill.

Prayers go up for Ernest. We wait for a miracle. But by the first signs of autumn, Ernest's condition worsens.

The days grow shorter, the nights cooler. Despite this pleasant change, my grief is never far away.

Late one evening, I sit alone in my living room, a rosy piece of sun streaming through the curtains. Outside, an occasional breeze blows from the north, ruffling the tiptop of the large tree in the front yard.

Until that moment, I have not noticed the leaves' colors have changed from summer green to a dazzling gold. (It's funny how we often miss beautiful things when we are focused on our problems.)

As I stare out the window, each gust of wind sends a shower of yellow leaves to the ground below. A lovely sight, it is. Yet I am somewhat startled at the realization that the glorious colors of autumn are actually nature's colors of death. This gives me a peculiar feeling. *Soon the tree will be barren,* I think. *Stripped, until its rebirth in spring.*

At once, my thoughts turn to Ernest. *Was his "death sentence" somehow related to the lovely golden leaves before me?* I wonder.

Some hidden force propels me out the front door. Frantically, I scoop a clump of leaves in my hands and fling them high above my head. I long to put them back on the tree, demand they stay there. But I can't.

My chest pounding, I lean back against the tree's trunk, a patch of sun falling across my lap. I put my head in my hands and weep.

In mid-October, Ernest and Mildred drive across town to spend a few days with us. Even though Ernest looks tired and frail, his spirits seem high.

After supper one evening, I find Ernest propped upright on the sofa, the lamp glowing above his head, his cheeks pale. Mildred sits at the piano, her fingers lightly playing the keys. It is a late-night kind of tune, slow and easy, and the sight of them there in the yellow light brings a sigh to my lips.

Soon Ernest captures the melody. Faintly at first. Then his rich baritone voice swells, rising and falling to the music, filling the room, sending a shiver up my spine.

In years past, Ernest sang professionally, traveling around with gospel quartets, Mildred an accompanist. Some kind of sight they must have been.

The last note fades; I applaud softly. "PaPaw," I call to him, "do you want to go and lie down now?"

He smiles. "Hey, this feels good right here. Come on in and join us."

I do, and for the next couple of hours he entertains me with stories about the growing-up years of his four children. Even though I've heard each one—down to the tiniest detail—dozens of times before, this night they take on new dimensions.

They are funnier. Richer. Sweeter. I know that Ernest is telling them for the last time.

In November, Ernest is admitted to the hospital, where a few days later he suffers a stroke, paralyzing a portion of his face. He cannot speak. He utters strange noises.

Through persistence—and patience—we learn to differentiate between the low rumbling tones he makes. He smiles, a victorious smile.

A week before Thanksgiving, the doctor tells us it won't be long now.

For hours, I watch Ernest's children taking turns sitting by the bed of their father, clutching his ashen hand, smoothing back his damp hair. They sing to him; feebly, he sings to them. They whisper, "We love you, Daddy." He nods knowingly. And Mildred is always there.

We schedule round-the-clock vigils. The nights are exhausting. We drink lots of coffee, staring out into the night, wishing, wondering, hoping.

A week later, Ernest draws his final breath, his family hovered around him. With no struggle, he closes his eyes and sleeps, yielding himself into the arms of his Lord.

The day after the funeral, I come home and walk to the towering tree in the front yard. One golden leaf is all that remains.

Reaching up, I touch the leaf, setting it free. As I do, the little leaf speaks to me about life and death. It says: *Life is but a season. Temporary. Fleeting. Death will surely come. But be encour-*

Death's Colors

aged! For with death comes a promise. The promise of spring. The advent of new life.

Suddenly, I feel a burst of strength. My sorrow becomes bearable. For there *is* another life to come . . . one that will never know the colors of death.

"For if we believe that Jesus died and rose again, even so them also which sleep in Jesus will God bring with him."
(1 Thessalonians 4:14, KJV)

Thank You, God, that death is but a doorway to eternal life.

Lose not a chance to waken love.
Charles Dickens, *Things That Never Die*

When Love Came Calling

I t was Valentine's Day, and my husband had a rare day off. I was not so fortunate. For two weeks, my job had been grueling. An urgent project often found me putting in twelve-hour days. So when the florist delivered a grand arrangement of a dozen red roses shortly after noon, my mood lifted. I opened the envelope and drew out the card. *Love always, Stan*, it read.

"How sweet," I said to myself, placing the large vase of flowers on my desk. The sight of the roses cheered me and filled me with anticipation for the evening. With our daughter visiting her grandparents in Mississippi, it'd be just the two of us. Something that hadn't happened in a long while.

At 3:30, the phone rang. "Are you leaving at four?" Stan wanted to know. I was. "Good," he said. "Steaks are on the grill."

The sun was softening as I drove home, one hand steadying the vase of flowers beside me. So lovely was their fragrance, I

found myself relaxing. Just ahead, a man who loved me waited.

As I drove in, I glimpsed Stan out on the deck beside the grill. He greeted me at the gate with a kiss. "Are you hungry?"

"Starving," I said, realizing I was. He led me into the house, where I couldn't believe my eyes. The dining room—normally reserved for special occasions—resembled an intimate restaurant. Glass and silver dishes sparkled beneath the warm glow of two slender red candles. Cloth napkins lay perfectly folded beside two china plates. Somewhere in the house, I heard the soft strains of Jackie Gleason's orchestra.

"It's beautiful," I gasped, placing the roses in the center of the impressive table.

What followed was a luscious four-course meal, all prepared by the loving hands of my sweetheart. As the candles burned lower, I felt all of the day's tension melt away. Dining with my husband of thirteen years, just being near him, hearing his voice, feeling his touch, tasting his food, filled me with a powerful longing and love for him, and at the same time, a profound knowledge of his love for me. It wasn't a new feeling, but one often ignored because of the hectic schedules we both lived by. As the soft, romantic music spilled into the little room, I knew I would remember this Valentine's Day forever.

Driving to work the next morning, I thought about the evening I'd just spent with my husband. And I sensed the Lord whisper, *That's how I want it to be between us.*

"What, Lord?" I asked, unsure what He meant. "A dozen

roses? A table bathed in candlelight and spread with good food? Love notes? An evening of intimate conversation?"

Yes, He said. *Every day I send you flowers, but you hardly ever notice. You have a book filled with my love letters, but weeks pass without your reading them. I prepare a table just for you and Me. And I wait for you. Yet some days you never even speak to Me.*

A shiver ran up my spine as His words touched the secret places of my heart. I wanted to stop the car and weep. How foolish I had been, often dismissing the gentle wooing of God. In my busy world of deadlines and demands, how many times had I left Him dining alone like a jilted lover?

Suddenly, on a busy toll road overflowing with commuters, I had an insatiable thirst for God, for a more intimate relationship with Him. Just the two of us. And I knew the choice was mine. Just as the choice is yours.

God has given us the freedom to decide how intimate our relationship with Him will be. *We* choose whether or not we will dine with Him. Like an anxious lover, He stands waiting, hoping that we desire Him as strongly as He desires us.

"I stand at the door and knock. If anyone hears my voice and opens the door, I will come in and eat with him, and he with me."

(Revelation 3:20, NIV)

Dear Lord, I want to know You as never before. Please be the lover of my soul.

There is just one way to bring up a child in the way he should go and that is to travel that way yourself.
Abraham Lincoln

Father's Tradition

hen I was growing up—along the banks of the mighty Mississippi River—the three things I remember most are these: my mother's unmatched ability to duplicate a store-bought dress on a sewing machine, my older sister's endless primping, and my father's rich baritone voice filling the house with serious-sounding prayers. At times, it seemed his prayers could be heard worldwide, so loud they rang in my young ears.

I'm sure it happened, but I don't remember a morning that my father's voice in prayer didn't waken me long before it was time to get dressed for school. And many were the days I despised his moanings and groanings. *Just let me sleep*, I cried to myself. It was not unusual for me to bolt out of bed and to the door, shutting it with such force I hoped he'd get the message that he was disturbing the peace. No chance. If anything, he prayed louder!

WHISPERS FROM HEAVEN

Daddy generally prayed alone in the mornings, but in the evening, after supper dishes were put away, he gathered us all together for a time of family prayer. No one could go to bed until we had all prayed. That's the way it was. Period. No arguing.

In spite of knowing this, there were times when I made a feeble attempt to alter tradition. I've been known to feign illness, amnesia, and deafness. But none of my shenanigans fooled Daddy. Eventually, I accepted this as a way of life.

Daddy wasn't perfect. Many of his imperfections have rubbed off on me. But day after day, night after night, Daddy's prayers went up. And of all the names he called during those prayers, the one I remember most was mine.

Back then, I failed to grasp the meaning of it all. What was the point of having family prayer every single night?

Now, with a daughter of my own to raise, I reflect back on those childhood days and understand. In those sweet moments of devotion, my father was planting seeds in the hearts of his little girls. And like the tiny acorn that falls to the earth, those seeds did not spring up overnight. Results took time.

But little by little, year after year, the seeds flourished; a tree grew up. Today, prayer is a common sound in my home. Daddy's plantings bore fruit, after all.

This was never so obvious to me as the day I heard a muffled voice coming from the study. Quietly, I crept around the corner, and there was my young child on her knees, praying. Beside her, in a jagged row, lay three baby dolls, their faces buried in the rug.

I stood for a moment in the shadows of her small sanctuary. Then I heard her say, "Lord, please bless my little children," as she patted each doll on the back.

I knew another tree was taking root.

"Blessed is the man that walketh not in the counsel of the ungodly, . . . he shall be like a tree planted by the rivers of water, that bringeth forth his fruit in his season."
(Psalm 1:1-3, KJV)

Raise up praying fathers among us, Lord.

*May there be enough clouds in our lives to make a
beautiful sunset.*
Rebecca Gregory

A Time of Refreshing

It was the last day of our summer vacation. I
stood silently at the edge of the little fishpond
behind my parents' house, watching Stan and
our daughter, Anna, fish. The past few weeks
at home had been dotted with unpleasant discoveries: a close
friend had been unfaithful to her husband; my sister—my con-
fidant for ten years—was moving to another city; my mother
was recovering from serious eye surgery.

The domino effect had taken its toll. I struggled with depres-
sion. My soul felt dry, wilted, in dire need of nourishment. As I
gazed over the pond's smooth water, its calmness seemed to mock
me.

I turned to go back to the house but spotted a pair of deer
tracks by the water's edge. *So what?* I thought. *Why should I
care?* But for some reason, I stopped, then turned to trace the
trail to the dense woods about a dozen yards away.

The tracks appeared fresh. Their shape and size suggested a

doe. No doubt this small pond was the deer's watering hole, bringing her down here several times a day to refresh herself from the summer's grueling heat.

Crouching down, I studied the tracks along the muddy bank. Nothing peculiar about them; just ordinary deer tracks. Yet an odd, joyful feeling washed over me, as if God had drawn me to this specific place to learn something. Whatever it was, I longed to know.

"What's that?" Stan asked, strolling up beside me. "Deer tracks?"

"I guess so," I said with a shrug.

He pointed across the water, where he had been fishing. "There's a whole bunch of them over there."

"They must be thirsty," I mumbled, more to myself than to anybody else. As quickly as I'd spoken those words, I thought of the Scripture verse in Psalms: "As the deer pants for streams of water, so my soul pants for you, O God" (Psalm 42:1, NIV).

I studied the tracks, my heart aching with a great heaviness I couldn't shake. I dipped my hand into the still, cool water. Something wonderful seemed to transpire with that single action. It was as though a gentle stream of water trickled its way into my being, restoring the dry places of my soul, reviving my spirits.

"Are you ready to go back?" Stan called. I nodded, grabbing a few lawn chairs and a fishing rod.

As we marched through the weeds back to the house, I sensed the deer tracks had been a message from God: When you are

devastated or disappointed, when burdens fall across your shoulders, come to the Source of strength that never runs dry. All I need do was make a path, like the tracks in the mud.

"He turneth the wilderness into a standing water, and dry ground into watersprings."
(Psalm 107:35, KJV)

Dear God, when we are parched, only You can quench our thirst.

He does most in God's great world who does his best in his own little world.
Thomas Jefferson

One Wednesday

On a dreary Wednesday morning, I sat behind the desk at the crisis pregnancy center wondering who would show up. Lately, I found myself second-guessing my decision to volunteer. After all, what could one woman possibly do to make a difference in the struggle against abortion anyway?

I had just settled in when the glass-paneled door opened an inch, then two. The girl on the other side appeared small and young. When she spoke, her voice was hushed. "Are you open?"

"Yes," I said, matching her whisper. "Come on in."

The petite girl stood trembling, her hands fumbling with the buttons on her white blouse. In a motherly fashion, I moved to her and draped my arm around her small shoulders. "Are you OK?"

With that, the girl put her head in her hands and sobbed. Gently, I led her into the inner office and helped her sit down in a chair. Offering her a box of tissues, I held her hand while she wept. I knew why she was crying. She was not much different from the others I see every Wednesday. She was pregnant— and scared half to death.

In a little while, her tears subsided. "I didn't mean to do that," she said apologetically.

"It's OK," I assured her. "I always feel better after a good cry. Don't you feel better?"

"Yeah," she said, relieved. "I do."

I patted her arm. "My name is Dayle, and I'm here to help you. If you want to talk, I'd love to listen."

She twisted the wilted tissue in her lap, ran a hand through frizzy blond hair, and got right to the point. "Well, my name is Lisa*; I'm seventeen, and I'm almost three months pregnant." Her voice faltered at the word *pregnant.*

"Has a doctor confirmed your pregnancy, Lisa?"

"Yeah," she said, her voice strangely confident.

"Do your parents know you're pregnant?"

"No."

"Does the father of the baby know you're pregnant?"

"Uh, yeah."

"And how did he react?"

"He wants me to have an abortion, but he doesn't have the money, so . . ."

"Lisa," I said softly. "I want you to know, first of all, that I believe in you. And I believe you're going to make it through this crisis. Right now, I know you're hurting. That's understandable, but I want you to have faith in yourself."

She rolled her eyes as if to say, "Yeah, right."

"I mean it," I assured her. "A lot of girls have sat in that chair, and I know you're going to be OK. We're here to help you." I touched her hand. She smiled.

After filling out the standard form I gave her, Lisa sat back and sighed, looking much too young to know anything about sex, let alone about having babies.

"Whatever choice you make," I told her, "please give it a lot of thought; we must live with our choices," I cautioned her. "Forever."

She eyed me curiously.

My heart ached for her. "What do you *want* to do, Lisa?"

"Well—right now, I think I want to have it," she said firmly. "I mean, it's *my* baby!" Then she looked worried. "But it would be so hard and everything."

"Would you consider adoption?"

"I don't know. I might."

"Do you think your parents will be supportive?"

She thought a minute. "I know they'll be hurt." Her lips quivered. "But they love me. So . . . yeah, I think they'll be OK."

I picked up one of the folders we give all our clients and flipped through it, explaining the various ways our organization could help her: finding good prenatal care at a reduced rate; a place to live; signing up for government assistance; free maternity clothes; free childbirth classes; adoption information.

I stopped and looked into her youthful eyes. "You know I can't make any decisions for you; I'm only hoping to help you make a *constructive* choice."

She nodded casually, as if I had just mentioned the price of beans.

"Would you like to see a film that shows the baby in the womb?" I asked cheerfully.

She smiled. "Yeah! That'd be cool."

Her answer brought a trace of hope.

As Lisa viewed the film, she appeared astonished. She uttered words like *wow* and *neat* whenever the baby jumped or flipped or sucked a thumb.

When the tape ended, Lisa stood and took the blue folder off the desk. "I'm gonna talk to my parents tonight," she announced, her voice steady.

"I think that's the right thing to do, Lisa. Would you like me to call you next week and see how you're doing?"

"Sure," she said cheerily.

I walked her to the door, then gave her a brief hug. "Take care of yourself," I told her.

She leaned back and rubbed her abdomen. "I'm gonna take care of this kid in here too," she said. "That's for sure."

It felt like a ton of bricks dropped off my shoulders. Reaching for the doorknob, Lisa paused briefly, her eyes turning to meet mine. "Thanks for being here" was all she said.

One Wednesday

I watched her small figure move down the hall toward the stairs. "God, give her courage," I whispered. At the corner, she turned and waved. I waved back, my inner strength returning. As I closed the door, Lisa's final words floated through the quiet room. *Thanks for being here . . .*

Something dawned on me: Even though I had doubted myself earlier, I—one ordinary woman—had made a difference. While I had not stood in an exalted place of power or jolted the earth with my philosophies, I *had* made a contribution. And I knew it was the way God intended. For He could not have, physically, sat in my chair today. He could not have held the trembling hand of a pregnant girl. If the door had been locked when Lisa arrived, God would not have opened it.

No. His earthly work depends on *people*. Ordinary people. People just like me and you, doing whatever we can to change our corner of the world.

"Let us not be weary in well doing: for in due season we shall reap, if we faint not."
(Galatians 6:9, KJV)

Help us, Lord, to be vessels today.

* Not her real name.

Great trials seem to be necessary preparation for great duties.
E. Thompson

A Test of Faith

t was 1921, a bittersweet year for young Oliver Fauss and his family. Not only was he pastoring a small congregation in Louisiana, he was also a "circuit rider," holding week-end meetings in several other small communities.

While seeing people give their lives to the Lord brought Oliver a great sense of satisfaction, he sometimes grew disheartened by uncontrollable circumstances.

He and his wife, Jewel, had no means of transportation, and often Oliver found himself having to walk to his weekend appointments. It wasn't unusual for this to mean a round trip of twenty-four miles on muddy roads, in a pair of shoes full of holes. (And we have problems driving to church twice a week.)

Nonetheless, Oliver did what had to be done. His little family depended on him to bring back enough home-grown vegetables, canned goods, and meager offerings from the saints to sustain them another week. But then there were times when

A Test of Faith

the Louisiana rains came with such force Oliver could not make the trip.

It had been one such weekend. Monday morning dawned and found the Fauss family with forty cents to last the week. Oliver knew God would provide somehow; He had provided many times before. It was now a matter of how.

With a hopeful heart, this faithful man of God took the hand of his small daughter, Rachel, and started for the store across the railroad tracks. At least he could buy oil for the lamp, a loaf of bread, and whatever bit the change would buy, he reasoned.

At the tracks a train sat, blocking the crossing. Oliver and Rachel walked about thirty yards to the rear of the train, intent on crossing there. Just as they reached the caboose, however, the train roared into life and pulled away, leaving the crossing clear. Oliver stood still for a moment, wondering why the conductor was operating the train in such a bizarre fashion.

As father and daughter turned to go back to the crossing, Oliver glanced down and saw something silver glinting on a crosstie. On closer inspection, he realized it was a silver dollar! He would later write, "It looked as big as a wagon wheel."

Oliver picked up the silver dollar and wept tears of gratitude all the way to the store. The great God of heaven had used a train on a railroad track to supply the needs of a poor preacher.*

WHISPERS FROM HEAVEN

"But my God shall supply all your need according to his riches in glory."
(Philippians 4:19, KJV)

Dear Lord, sometimes the obstacles before us hold the answers we desperately seek. Help us look closely for them.

*O. F. Fauss, *What God Hath Wrought: The Complete Works of O. F. Fauss* (Hazelwood, Mo.: Word Aflame Press, 1985).

Wrinkles should merely indicate where smiles have been.
Mark Twain

Change—Friend or Foe?

ot long ago, I stood in front of the bathroom mirror squinting and plucking at a new crop of gray hairs. My husband walked in and asked, "What are you doing?"

"I'm pulling out gray hairs," I said. "Isn't it depressing?"

"What? Gray hairs? Not particularly, no."

I glanced at his full head of hair, loaded with gray. He looked handsome. "Not depressing for you," I said. "You look great with yours; I look downright ugly."

"Don't be silly," he said. "You could never be ugly." With that impulsive promise, he planted a kiss square on the top of my graying head.

I stepped back from the mirror. "Are you telling me that when I am eighty-six years old with a flabby potbelly and prickly hairs on my chin that you will say I'm . . . *pretty?*" I did not think it funny; he laughed uproariously.

"If you have hair on your chin," he said, "you can borrow my razor. Besides, you're making an issue over nothing."

"It isn't nothing," I argued. "And I'm not making an issue over it."

He shrugged. "Why are you so worried about this? You can't avoid getting old. Why not just accept it?"

Of course, he was right. This wasn't a discussion about gray hairs and flabby bodies; it was about accepting change.

My husband has always been a level-headed person. The unavoidable seldom bothers him. He is one who goes with the flow, taking life as it comes.

Not me.

I first discovered my tendency to argue with the unavoidable in the ninth grade. My English teacher, Mr. Henson, handed me an autobiography of Edward VIII and said, "I want an oral and written report on this next Thursday."

Mr. Henson was a breed of his own. He dipped, he chewed—in class!—he dragged his fingernails across the blackboard to hear the girls scream, and he stank. Whenever you were caught chewing gum, he made you stick the stuff on your nose and walk circles around the room until the bell rang. If you daydreamed in class, you had to stand in the hall. The only hitch was you had to keep your hand on a blue square painted on the wall. If your hand fell off the blue square, you got swats.

After that assignment was given, I stomped to Mr. Henson's desk and announced, "It's not fair!"

"What's not fair?" he said, flashing his tobacco-stained teeth.

Change—Friend or Foe?

"This!" I roared, waving the formidable three-inch book in his face. "You gave everyone in the class an easy assignment except me. Why?"

"Because I like you," he said. "And I'm the teacher. Now get outta here!"

After I pouted and whined for two days, Mr. Henson finally gave in and let me select the book of my choice. So maybe I have Mr. Henson to blame for my habit of fighting the inevitable. Maybe I left ninth grade convinced that with enough finagling, enough bargaining, enough negotiating, I could charter a course in life free of unpleasant events. I had always hoped this to be true.

But over the years, I've learned better. You might even say I've managed to become a friend of change. I've come to see it as part of God's master plan. In the face of a grave illness—when all that could be done had been done—instead of resisting, I've cried out in surrender and uncovered enormous courage. At the death of a loved one, instead of trying to hang on, I've chosen to let go, discovering a peace I didn't think possible.

Change forces me to expose a delicate area of myself, yet I've found that when I liberate that buried emotion, acceptance of my predicament follows; the way becomes amazingly clear. Strange, isn't it?

So now I stood gazing long and hard at three gray hairs lying in the sink. I studied my aging face in the mirror. Would I accept it—or reject it? It was a test.

WHISPERS FROM HEAVEN

With little effort I could have rushed out to the drugstore, bought a bottle of chemicals, and poured them on my hair. I could have scheduled collagen injections for the "laugh lines" scattered about my face. But how long could I keep up the charade? Five years? Ten?

Taking a brush, I smoothed back my rumpled hair, knowing the grays would be back in a couple of weeks. Reaching to put out the light, I hesitated. On impulse, I smiled. Tiny wrinkles gathered around my eyes—like a row of faithful friends.

"Beauty is vain: but a woman that feareth the Lord, she shall be praised."
(Proverbs 31:30, KJV)

Seasons change, Lord. Help me to change as gracefully as they.

The beginning of anxiety is the end of faith.
George Mueller

Clouds of Doubt

ith an annoyed eye, I studied the inky clouds thickening over the Houston skyline as I steered the car through the crowded downtown streets. Oblivious to the threat of bad weather, my little daughter, Anna, sat beside me, humming a happy tune. I envied her carefree existence. Running errands is not a favorite pastime of mine, certainly not in Houston's evening traffic during a downpour. But that was not my main concern this day.

For several weeks, I had been brooding over my husband's upcoming promotional test. The Lord knew we needed this promotion. And I had prayed about it. But, like a frightened child, I needed reassurance that all would be well.

So while I inched through the crowded avenues of the city, I fretted fiercely. If my husband didn't get this promotion, we might have to sell our home; tax increases had caused our payment to jump about $200 a month. Stan would be testing with several hundred people; only a handful would make the grade. And due to our city's budget cuts, this was to be the last such promotional exam for some time. All that aside, my husband had given many years to his job; he deserved this promotion. The farther I drove, the more I worried.

Suddenly, Anna cried, "Look, Mama! There's Jesus in the clouds!"

I nearly lost control of the car, afraid I was missing the second coming.

"What?" I shouted, jerking back to my lane of traffic.

"Look up, Mama!" she urged, her finger pointing, her face shining. "There's *Jesus!* See?"

Only then did I realize that my little daughter—the one who is always finding delightful pictures in the clouds—had found the image of Jesus. Speechless, I stared straight ahead and, sure enough, there it was, in the murky skies above me: A perfect profile of Jesus Christ.

Tears sprang, unannounced, to my eyes. For the past thirty minutes—the past month!—I had been focused on problems, fearing the unknown, when all the while Jesus, the problem solver, was in the clouds. It was a most stirring discovery.

As I watched the little cloud break away, I breathed His name: "Jesus." Immediately, it seemed the Lord whispered to me, *I've been here all along; don't be afraid.*

Under a steady rain, I drove home comforted. Stan did get the promotion, but I learned a valuable truth that day. What-

Clouds of Doubt

ever weather life sends me—be it sunny or stormy—one thing remains sure: God *is* always there.

> *"The eyes of the Lord are over the righteous."*
> (1 Peter 3:12, KJV)

Help me, Lord, to remember that no cloud is dark enough to hide me from You.

What is lovely never dies, but passes into other loveliness.
Tomas Bailey Aldrich, *A Shadow of the Night*

Lori's Legacy

ori's gone." It was the voice of my mother calling from Mississippi early one September morning.

"Gone? You mean she's dead?" I asked, not wanting to know the answer.

But it was true. After fighting for two years, this precious four-year-old soldier, Lori Moore, had died from cancer. She and my daughter were the same age.

Even though Anna had only been with Lori once—and that was when they were both about eight months old—I had kept her posted on Lori's struggle with cancer. Together, we prayed for Lori; she kept Lori's picture on her dresser at all times. She always called Lori her friend.

When I mustered up the courage to tell Anna about Lori's death, I called her into the room. She had never looked so beautiful as I took her little hands in mine and said, "Sweetheart, I have some very sad news." She waited. "Lori died last night."

Lori's Legacy

Silently, she stared unbelievingly into my eyes. Then, in a weak voice, her lips trembling, she said, "Are you sure?" All I could do was nod my head yes. Falling against me, Anna wept. "Oh, Mother," she sobbed, "Lori was such a *special* little girl."

Indeed she was. In her hometown of Jackson, Mississippi, Lori had captured the hearts of many in her struggle for survival. A total of $140,000 had been donated by citizens from all over Mississippi. It went to pay for the bone-marrow transplant Lori underwent at Egleston's Children's Hospital in Atlanta, Georgia, in 1989. And now, the battle was over. Lori was gone.

This unsettling news devastated me. Lori's mom, Ruth, and I had been childhood friends. I loved her like a sister. How could such a tragedy happen? For several days, I found myself unable to do little besides cry. Especially when I looked at the cherubic face of my little daughter. It all seemed so unfair.

Several weeks after Lori's death, Ruth wrote to me. "It's been a month today," she penned, "and the emptiness is almost unbearable." Even though miles of roads separated us, reading these words brought a terrible ache to my heart. The vast emptiness she spoke of I could only imagine.

Later in the week, I decided to visit the local arboretum. Already the leaves had started to change colors, and the chrysanthemums were in full bloom. In the center of the park, sunny benches circled a great fountain, spraying and spewing crystal drops of water over a mound of white rocks.

I strolled over and sat down, watching the sun slip behind

silvery clouds. Sitting there, I felt so in tune with God. It was His world. He was here, now, on this bench with me. I could see Him in the leaves dancing along the sidewalk, hear Him in the water as it splashed to the rocks below, feel Him in the wind that ruffled my hair. I was alone with God.

Resting my head on the back of the little bench, I let the tears fall. Whether or not anyone saw me didn't matter. For the most part of an hour, I stayed on the bench and cried. I cried for all the pain Lori had endured in her short life; for all the times she couldn't run and play with her big brother, Rick, because she was held captive in a hospital bed. I cried for the loss in Rick's life; for the sister he will never see grow up. I cried for the sleepless days and nights of Lori's parents, Ruth and Ricky; the nights when they must have stared at the ceiling above them while their hearts screamed, "Why?" I cried for all the people in Lori's life who would miss her dearly. And I cried because the void she left will never be completely filled.

At last, I dug in my pocket for the tissues I'd brought. A gardener walked toward me. "The park closes in ten minutes," he said. I blew my nose and started to leave, when my eyes fell on a square of orange and red chrysanthemums, their heads nodding lazily in the evening breeze. As I drank in their loveliness, the thought struck me: *These flowers will fade. Each petal will wither and drop to the earth. To the human eye, they will appear dead. But mums are perennials; they pale, only to return year after year.*

Lori's Legacy

I thought of Lori, so lovely, once so full of life, and it seemed the Lord tapped me on the shoulder and said: *Don't grieve. She will bloom again.*

This thought brought a bittersweet sigh to my lips. I reached down and plucked a single red mum. Its perfection would serve as a reminder of the legacy Lori left behind and of sweeter days to come.

"Suffer the little children to come unto me, and forbid them not: for of such is the kingdom of God."
(Mark 10:14, KJV)

O great God of love, our finite minds cannot understand why little children must die. But we know that when these things come to us, You will be there to carry us through.

To the man who himself strives earnestly, God also lends a helping hand.
Aeschylus

Helping Hands

hirley Moon will never forget Mother's Day, 1979. She and her husband, Jerry, and their thirteen-month-old son piled into their old Chevrolet and headed out.

As they rolled along under a canopy of blue skies, thinking about the barbecue dinner waiting at her brother's house, Shirley glanced down at her little son and smiled. This was her second year to be a mother, and nothing was going to spoil this day.

But that was before the car died at the red light. "Not this again," she mumbled to herself, remembering all the other times they'd sat at red lights in a lifeless car.

While Jerry attempted to start the Chevy, Shirley longed to be rid of the junker forever. But it was only wishful thinking. At eighteen, and with minimum-wage jobs, another car was completely out of the question. They did well to buy diapers.

All at once, the carburetor backfired fiercely, a cloud of smoke rose ominously from under the hood. It wasn't unusual behavior for the Chevy. Jerry had seen it happen many times before.

Resignedly, he crawled out to take a look. As he raised the hood, flames rushed out to meet him. Ripping off his shirt, Jerry tried to smother the blaze but soon realized he couldn't. He yelled for Shirley to get the baby and run.

Grabbing the baby and her personal belongings, Shirley raced up the steep embankment toward the freeway. Standing there clutching her small son, watching their only car going up in smoke, she was consumed with an awful sense of hopelessness.

"Help us, God," she prayed, looking up and down the freeway for somebody to help them. But there was no traffic.

When it seemed hope was gone, a man ran up carrying a fire extinguisher and, in a flash, put the fire out. Jerry turned to thank him, but the man was gone. No one saw where he came from, and no one saw where he went.

When the car was towed home, Jerry vacuumed out the residue from the extinguisher, put in a new set of wires and hoses, adjusted the timing, and cranked it up. The car ran for another year before they put in a new engine. Shirley is convinced the man with the fire extinguisher was their guardian angel.

"He shall give his angels charge over thee, to keep thee in all thy ways."
(Psalm 91:11, KJV)

When our world is going up in smoke, Lord, send an angel our way.

Earth has no sorrow that Heaven cannot heal.
Thomas Moore, "Come, Ye Disconsolate"

Questions and Answers

"I s God an old man?" my daughter, then four, asks on the way home from church one afternoon.

I repeat the question, buying time. "The Bible says God is a Spirit," I tell her. "He's always been and always will be. God is not young or old."

He is to her. "Is Him *six* or *twelve?*" she asks emphatically, as if it has to be one or the other.

She is packed with questions and answers these days. The experts tell me it has something to do with being four. One minute she knows nothing, only to know it all the next. But four is also the age of budding independence. No longer does she blindly accept my every word as truth.

At the dinner table one evening, Anna suddenly remembers the mongoloid girl we saw at the library yesterday. "Why that little girl not look like a little girl?" she asks.

Her round face seems more precious, more perfect, than ever

Questions and Answers

as I conjure up images of the Down's syndrome child wearing a tight red shirt and short blue pants, drool spilling from her bottom lip.

"That little girl was born that way," I tell her. "Just because people look different doesn't make them . . ."

She interrupts. "Will her always be like that?"

"Yes, baby, I'm afraid she will."

My answer disturbs her; she finishes her meal with a forlorn face.

I sit quietly, thinking about this universal need for answers. From childhood to awkward adolescence, through the turbulent teens and into our adult lives, our paths are dotted with whys and what ifs. We're compelled to seek answers.

Often, I listen as friends vow to carry a list of questions with them to heaven's gate. So anxious they are to know the reason for this or for that: Why did my mother die? Why did my business go bankrupt, leaving me penniless? Why did my husband desert his family? How could my wife leave me for another man?

Seeking the answers to such perplexing questions seems to usher them onward, toward the day they can finally ask why. "God, *why?*"

As I pray with Anna beside her bed that night, she prays for the Down's syndrome girl. During our good-nights, she sits up in bed and says, "Her *won't* always look like that, Mommy," as if she finally solved a puzzle.

I kiss her forehead, letting my lips linger.

"Not in heaven," she says. It's not a question now. She has the answer.

"There shall be no more death, neither sorrow, nor crying, neither shall there be any more pain: for the former things are passed away."
(Revelation 21:4, KJV)

Thank You, Lord, for the hope of a world without questions.

This is not altogether a golden world, but there are countless gleams of gold to be discovered in it if we give our minds to them.
Henry Alford Porter

Golden Threads

t would be fun. After four years of staying at home raising my daughter and pursuing other interests, part-time work sounded exciting. During the demanding years of dirty diapers and sleepless nights, I often thought about reentering the job force. It would be a freeing experience, I concluded. So I hired a friend to sit with Anna, signed with an agency, and eagerly accepted the assignment for Friday.

The job proved uneventful until a zealous young man with bad breath approached my desk. In his hand, he balanced a stack of papers about two inches thick. He introduced himself as "Bruce."

"Look," he said, sighing and scratching his head. "I need to get this document copied."

"Fine," I said. "No problem."

"It's about two hundred pages long." Bruce flicked the mound of papers for my benefit. "And I need ten copies of each page."

WHISPERS FROM HEAVEN

He scratched his head again. "Hmm. That's about two thousand copies, isn't it?" He looked worried. "It was supposed to be ready at noon; there's a meeting with," he dropped his voice an octave, " 'the big boys' at three."

I glanced at my watch. 1:00. Clearly, a rush job.

"Fine," I said. "No problem." (I do love challenges!)

Bruce trailed me down the hall and into a small copy room. Fortunately, this copier could do it all—including laundry on Thursdays. *Unfortunately*, it took an instant disliking to me. Or maybe it was the wiry young man named Bruce who insisted on overseeing the entire operation—bad breath and all.

Whichever the case, the copier refused to work. And so, after twenty minutes of interpreting error codes, trying and failing, we both decided to try the copier upstairs.

It worked, but before I had copied five minutes, the door of the room burst open, and in swooped a tall, dark-haired woman, shrieking, "STOP THAT COPIER! STOP THAT COPIER!"

Startled, I retreated a couple of steps, unsure if this was a holdup for paper clips or an informal staff meeting. Seeing my stunned expression, the middle-aged woman said in a hushed voice, "I'm sorry, but Mr. K is waiting on these, and they must be copied *now.*"

Hurriedly, I collected my two hundred–page document and backed out of the way while she took over. Obviously, Mr. K had a great deal of influence around the place—at least on the woman making his copies.

Golden Threads

When she left, I stacked my "rush job" in the collator and punched the "start" button. That's when the door swung wide, and in strolled a stern-faced woman with red hair. I smiled, but she didn't. "Pardon me," she said curtly. "I have to get these copies made." As if *I* were there for an ice-cream soda.

Without a word, I shuffled the document together (page order in total disarray by now), backed away from the machine, and watched while she worked.

When at last she finished, the woman eyed me disapprovingly and coldly asked, "What department are *you* with?"

I resisted the awful temptation to say "hazardous waste" and said I was only there for the day—a temporary assignment.

"You're not supposed to be using this copier," she said, rebuking.

"I'm sorry, ma'am." I shrugged. "I'm just following Bruce's instructions."

"I'll have a word with Bruce," she snapped, and breezed out of the room, leaving me with my rush job.

The highlight of the day was when I walked—no, ran—into Bruce's office at 2:55 carrying two thousand copies in a box. Bruce looked as if he would faint. Grabbing the box from my hands, he asked, "Are you available next week? You're wonderful!"

I smiled. "Thank you, Bruce," I said. "I'll let you know." It was all I could muster.

On the way home, I said a prayer for all working mothers—

those who don't want to work outside the home but have no choice and those who work because they want to. How they managed to stay sane, I didn't know.

When I arrived at the house wilted, hot, and hungry, I was pleased that my husband had started dinner. It smelled delicious. But as we sat down to eat, I said a dreadful thing. "Looks like you got the broccoli a little too done," I told him.

My little daughter implored, "Mama, why can't you be happy with what you got—a good husband and somepin' to eat?"

For a moment, I was stunned. She was quite right. Why couldn't I? I looked at my family. They smiled. I smiled.

As we blessed the food, I realized how often I allow trivial things to pester me: a man with bad breath; a quirky copier; a rush job; a rude woman; overcooked vegetables. All the while, I had disregarded the golden threads God weaves daily into my life. It is those things that really count.

"Blessed be the Lord, who daily loadeth us with benefits."
(Psalm 68:19, KJV)

Lord, in my hustle-and-bustle world, I sometimes overlook the gold threads. Remind me again.

*What we have done for ourselves alone dies with us; what we
have done for others and the world remains and is immortal.*
Albert Pike

Gifts From Grandmother

ix days before Christmas, I received word that
my maternal grandmother was dead. A heart
attack. So suddenly, so unexpectedly snatched
away.

I was filled with an enormous sense of loss. Not just for me
but for my young daughter, as well. Never will Grandmother be
a real part of her life. Only a strange face to study in a photo-
graph album. For this, I grieved.

As I lay across the bed, struggling to make sense of it all,
images of this dear woman flashed before me. I wept uncon-
trollably. For it was Christmas, and Grandmother was dead.

Without a doubt, Grandmother's house was a special place,
especially during the holiday season. As a young child, I remember anxiously waiting for the appointed day when our
family would pile into the car and head toward northern Mississippi for Christmas at my grandparents' house.

After what seemed like an eternity, we'd drive up, plunge out of the car, and wrap ourselves around Grandmother's stocky frame, burying our faces in her freshly starched housedress. Laughing, she would guide us into the kitchen, where the pressure cooker sat hissing, sending the divine smell of fresh turnip greens or purple hull peas wafting through the house.

Furtively, my sisters and I would roam from room to room, hoping to catch a glimpse of gaily wrapped packages with our names on them.

It never happened.

Grandmother believed in the element of surprise. We knew the gifts were there. And she knew we knew. But, without fail, she waited until the final moment, when our emotions skyrocketed, before she revealed the whereabouts of the hidden prizes.

Breathlessly, I'd settle on the sofa listening to the rustle of her garments as she ambled down the long hall. In a few minutes, she'd return, bearing the coveted gifts.

"Well—look what I found," she'd say, her voice childlike, her face glowing like a southern sunset.

As she handed me my gift, I'd grin knowingly as I meekly accepted her offering, my heart beating wildly.

Yes, I fondly remember those days. But more than any Christmas package, I recall the countless times I heard Grandmother pray; heard her call out each child's name, an urgency in her voice. And I see her standing behind the podium of the little church in Mississippi, a Bible in her hands, as she fervently delivered the morning message. "God is good!" she would say, her voice high and lifted up.

At the funeral home, I stumbled to the open casket. She looked asleep. Some thoughtful person had placed a lovely bouquet of flowers in her hands. Each delicate petal painfully reminded me of the fragility of this life. A vapor, no less.

Reaching out to caress her silent form, I found myself overcome by my mourning. *How could I ever celebrate Christmas without Grandmother?* I wondered. And then, just as quickly, I realized I didn't have to.

My observance of Christ's birthday is not locked into one day of the year; I celebrate His birth every day. So it is with Grandmother. Her life could not be left lying in some cold blue box, only to be remembered on the anniversary of her death or her birth. A part of Grandmother will *always* be with me.

For the gifts she gave during her lifetime will never decay with the passing of time; they are eternal.

"We know that if our earthly house of this tabernacle were dissolved, we have a building of God, an house not made with hands, eternal in the heavens."
(2 Corinthians 5:1, KJV)

Lord, we anxiously await that great reunion in the sky.

Whatever your despair or your frustration—this, too, will pass.
Grace Noll Crowell, *This, Too, Will Pass*

A Season and a Promise

a-aa-ma!" Anna stands outside peering in the bay window, her hands and face pressed snugly against the glass. "Come here!" she calls.

I am sprawled on the sofa in the living room. "Get your hands off the window," I say, scolding.

"Mama, I need you to come here," she says, her breath fogging up the pane.

"Anna, can't you see I am resting? My back's killing me. Please, go swing."

She frowns but doesn't budge.

"Look what you're doing to the window," I tell her, my voice testy.

"Ma'am?" She presses her ear to the window.

"The window. Look at it. Daddy just cleaned it yesterday." I am shouting.

Retreating one step, Anna puts her hands on her hips and

says, "Mama, this is real important. Come look at what I found. It's a surprise."

"No," I say firmly. "I'm gonna lay here awhile. Maybe I'll be out in a few minutes." I feel like a beastly mother, ignoring my child's call to adventure, and yet I can't bring myself to move.

With a dejected look, Anna scuttles off toward the great maple tree in the backyard, leaving her smudgy prints on the glass and an ache in my heart.

It is the first time she's been out to play in several weeks. Winter has finally struck Texas, ushering in cold drizzles and a hard freeze. The yard lies desolate, depressing. No color. No foliage. No life. So when I spied strips of rosy sun stretching across the bedroom floor this morning, I bundled my daughter from head to toe and shooed her out the door. She would play while I rested.

The past two months have found me grappling with back pain—something I've done off and on for most of my adult life. The problem stems from a number of things—all out of my control. At times, the pain is almost unbearable. Take it easy and stay in bed, the doctor tells me. But how does a mother of a preschooler do such a thing? In spite of Anna's valiant attempts to help me, she can't understand the extent of my discomfort. Just getting out of bed is often an effort. When the pain worsens, my mood plummets. Today, I have reached a point where hopelessness reigns. I long for relief.

Gazing out at the naked trees, I watch my daughter dawdle

in the dirt beneath the maple. This towering tree is a beauty in summer. Its boughs, heavy with leaves, provide an oasis of shade for my family. Now it stands barren, stripped, its branches painfully stark.

In a minute, Anna is back at the window. "Come look, Mama!" she yells. "Quick!"

It sounds urgent, but I know every timbre of my daughter's voice so well. This is pure excitement. Probably nothing more than an ant traveling south. I pretend to be asleep. Maybe she'll go away.

She doesn't. "Mama! Get up! *Please!*" Her small voice lifts with each sentence.

How can I resist such a persuasive plea? Even the most dreadful mothers have a breaking point. Warily, I shuffle across the carpeted floor and out the back door, holding on to my aching back. A blast of winter's wind stings my eyes.

Anna beams when she sees me. Standing there, parka framing her small head, her face resembles a hooded street lamp.

"Over here, Mama." She waves her arms about her head, her breath making flimsy clouds. "You won't believe it!"

With sluggish movements, I plod to the foot of the tree and stare down at the lawn. Once plush and green, it now crunches under my feet, prickly and brown. "What is it, sweetie? What do you want to show me?"

"Right there, Mama," she says, barely above a whisper.

"Right where?"

A Season and a Promise

"Look—right there."

I look down in the direction she points, but I see nothing except cold, hard ground. "What? Where?" I ask, feeling foolish.

Without speaking, Anna drops to her knees—almost reverently—and gently touches something. She glances back over her shoulder at me but says nothing. Her round face takes on an ethereal quality.

Not wanting to break the spell, I crouch beside her, closely inspecting the ground. And then I see it—pushing up through the bitter earth is the fresh green shoot of a jonquil.

I am awed. Like my daughter, I am unable to speak. *How?* I wonder. *How could it be coming up now? Jonquils aren't due for another month—or two.* But it is there. In the palm of winter's icy hand, surrounded by total barrenness, a sprig of green stands straight as an arrow. I know in a few weeks the jonquil will be in full bloom, its yellow head bobbing in the breeze.

Despite the fact that I am wearing my pink chenille bathrobe and my hair is slightly askew, the moment seems sacred, God's presence near.

I think of the scripture verse: "To everything, there is a season." *Season.* The word comforts me somehow. For I realize that seasons not only have beginnings but *endings*, each one having served its purpose. We travel from summer's grueling heat to winter's biting cold, enjoying the pleasant—enduring the unpleasant.

WHISPERS FROM HEAVEN

For a moment, I ponder this. Yes, life is made up of seasons—blissful seasons; seasons of anguish; prosperous seasons; seasons of want. Like winter's chill, none of them is permanent. And they all serve a purpose in the life of a child of God. "We know that all things work together for good to them that love God" (Romans 8:28, KJV).

All things. I think of my back.

Kneeling in the dirt with my daughter, I sense God has brought me to the foot of this barren tree to give me hope: *Whenever you find yourself in the midst of a bitter season, remember the jonquil. Spring will come. And nothing can stop it!*

A chilly wind sweeps across the yard, ruffling the tip of the green sprig. I turn to Anna and pull her close. She seems to read my heart and holds me for a long while, the afternoon sun wrapping around us like a warm blanket.

"The God of all grace, who called you to his eternal glory in Christ, after you have suffered a little while, will himself restore you and make you strong, firm and steadfast."
(1 Peter 5:10, NIV)

Just when our winters seem endless, Lord, You send us the spring.

*I would rather walk with God in the dark than go alone
in the light.*
Mary G. Brainard

Promises in the Sand

After almost forty years in the mission field, Sallie Bargo figured she had seen it all. But nothing could have prepared her for the tragic death of her daughter in an automobile accident. For Sallie and her husband, Herb, time stood still. No words could match their pain.

Shortly after their daughter's untimely death, a friend of Sallie's approached her and offered her the use of a condominium near the ocean. She encouraged Sallie to go for as long as she needed to. Just to get away and commune with God. Finally, Sallie agreed to go—but only if her friend went with her.

When they arrived, Sallie suggested they take a walk, along separate paths, each seeking a word from the Lord. They would share their experiences over dinner that evening.

A beach in November is a lonely place to be. But its vast emptiness could not equal the hole in Sallie's heart. Trudging through the white sand, the wind on her back, she poured out a grief-stricken soul to her Maker. "Father, please show me, somehow, that I will make it through this horrible place. Please, Father, I need to know that everything is going to be all right."

The farther Sallie walked, the heavier her load. If God created this wonderful universe, this magnificent beach, surely He could show her a sign today, a sign of hope, of peace. Finally, for some reason, she said, "Lord, please show me a complete, whole sand dollar. Let me find a whole sand dollar as a sign that everything's going to be all right."

Through tears of anguish, Sallie combed the beach, desperate to find the sand dollar. But she found none whole; only bits and pieces. Exhausted, she made her way back, her feet slow, her shoulders drooping.

Arriving at the condo, her friend rushed to meet her. "Sallie," she exclaimed, "I had the most wonderful experience! But you'll have to wait till dinner, like we agreed."

When dinner at last was prepared, Sallie listened in amazement as her friend shared her experience out on the beach:

"As I walked along the beach, I began to just praise God. Praises bubbled up out of me. It was while I was singing and praising the Lord that I saw this elderly couple walking toward me. Wanting to share the Lord, I approached them and learned they were both Christians.

"After we talked for a while, I told them why I was here at the beach—about you and your daughter's death. They both were so touched. The gentleman looked at his wife and said, 'I want to do something for Sallie. Give me a shell.' Reaching into her shoulder bag, the woman pulled out a lovely shell. He studied it a moment, then handed it back. 'I don't want to give her this one,' he said. 'Give me one of those sand dollars you found.' At once, the wife pulled out a sand dollar—whole and complete. He handed it to me and said, 'Here, give this to Sallie and tell her it is a sign that everything is going to be all right.' "

That was a number of years ago, and Sallie Bargo will never forget the experience. She believes that had *she* found the whole sand dollar, the enemy might have planted seeds of doubt in her mind, calling it mere coincidence. But because a complete stranger sent the whole sand dollar to her, using the exact words she had spoken to God, she says she *knew* God had heard her in her time of despair.*

"The Lord is nigh unto them that are of a broken heart."
(Psalm 34:18, KJV)

Lord, when my life has been shattered, You are there to make it whole again.

*Related by E. R. Webb, a co-worker at Compaq Computer in Houston, Texas, via electronic mail, 1993.

*If it were not for God who has felt as I've felt, I know I would
ache so much more than I do.*
Mary A. Kloepper, *Mirror of My Soul**

Letting Go of Things Precious

here is no kettle steaming. No pink sun streaming through the blinds. I feel a sick feeling in the pit of my stomach as I grope to silence the screaming alarm clock.

Today's the day, I think to myself. Drowsily, I crawl out of bed, creep into the next room, and stare down at my five-year-old daughter, one little hand crumpled under her cheek, her hair fanned out on the pillow.

In the light of the street lamp, I see a plaid jumper and white blouse hanging from the dresser drawer handle. "Put it right there, Mama," Anna had said the night before, "so I can jump up and get it on tomorrow. I can't be late for my first day at school." So great was her excitement I found myself cheering her on.

Was "tomorrow" already here? Last night, we were laughing and talking about all the things she would do at school; the people she would meet; the fun she would have. But tomorrow has arrived and, suddenly, all I want to do is tiptoe away from her bed, crawl back under my covers, and weep hysterically.

Grow up, I chide myself. *This is life. It is called "letting go."* Inwardly, I know every parent experiences school-day jitters, but at this moment I feel totally detached. And petrified.

Daylight peeks through the blinds as I kneel beside Anna's bed and offer a prayer for her safekeeping. I think of Hannah and the sacred vow she made to deliver back to God the son she so desperately desired. Childless, she could not have known the pain involved in such a commitment.

I try to imagine how Hannah's heart must have ached as she loaded Samuel's little things into a bag and prepared for the journey to the temple, the place of surrendering her young son to God.

When she embraced him that final time and watched his small form disappear inside, surely she felt a little like me at this moment: proud, yet devastated. For how could Hannah have known the end result: her young Samuel, a mighty prophet of God? What would have happened had Hannah not willingly surrendered her son to the Lord's keeping?

My natural instinct is to slap a stubborn grip on my little one; to tighten the reins. To forever shield her from anything resembling change. But this, I cannot do. I must change *with* change. I must loosen the reins a bit.

The mere thought is unsettling. But then, I remember Samuel hearing the voice of God in the night; Samuel prophesying to

Eli; Samuel becoming a great prophet in Israel; Samuel anointing David as Israel's king. He did all of this—and much more—because his mother let him go.

Martin Luther once said, "I have tried to keep things in my hands and lost them all, but what I have given into God's hands, I still possess." Sobering words, yet soothing words. At the schoolhouse, I kiss my Anna goodbye and watch her familiar form scuttle into the classroom, into the magnificent world of learning, of instructions and decisions, of friends and foes. She turns and waves to me, unaware of my inner turmoil.

Back in the car, I wipe a flow of tears from my face.

But I also take solace in the fact that my daughter does not really belong to me at all; she belongs to God. And, without a doubt, whatever is His, He is fully able to take care of.

That is awfully good news to a wobbly mother.

"The Lord will perfect that which concerneth me."
(Psalm 138:8, KJV)

There is a time to clutch and a time to let go. Father, help me to know the difference.

* Used, by permission, from *Mirror of My Soul*. Excerpt from "Changes" by Mary Kloepper.

It is easier to build temples of gold than to be temples of the Holy Ghost.
Anonymous

Holy Awakenings at Christmas

On Thursday morning, the first week of December, I hauled the dusty Christmas boxes from the attic and set out to fill our home with the holiday spirit. Eager as a child in a candy store, I flung open cartons, inspected breakables, and gently removed the dilapidated Nativity from its nest of white tissue paper. Slowly, I counted each ragged piece, assembled it, lovingly placed it on one end of the hearth, and dared anyone to touch it.

Although this particular Nativity is probably the least expensive item in my growing collection of Christmas decorations, its worth is immeasurable to me. My mother grew up with this cardboard creche; I grew up with this cardboard creche. At least fifty years old, it continues to bring me pleasure year after year. As a young girl, I can still remember crouching in front of the manger scene, my eyes mesmerized by the Virgin Mary. Wrapped in a pale blue robe, a glow about her head, she appeared beautiful to me. And so holy.

Smiling at the familiar faces of the shepherds and wise men, I steadied them in their corner of the stable, giving each a gentle pat. The beloved Nativity now belonged to me and my daughter.

Later in the day, I showed the manger scene to Anna—who was eighteen months old at the time—and painstakingly related the splendid story of Christmas, using the paper figures to illustrate the narrative.

Anna pointed to the wise men.

"Those are the three wise men," I said. "They've come to bring Baby Jesus gifts. See?" Holding up a cardboard wise man, I let her inspect the small parcel in his hand. Satisfied, she scooted off my lap and down the hall.

Over the next couple of days, I draped the house with trinkets and fresh holly; with wreaths and berry-scented candles, creating the cozy, country charm I find so appealing. I felt quite pleased with my talents.

Sunday afternoon, I dashed through the house—gathering up the few things I'd not used in my decorating spree—and found Sunshine lying at the edge of the manger scene. Sunshine is Anna's shabby doll, the one she loves more than all her toys combined. This is evident from the doll's frazzled appearance. Drooping eyelids. Limp body. One wiry strand of hair left.

This was not the first time I'd found the doll in the creche. Clearly, something must be done. Glancing at my daughter, I inquired, "What is Sunshine doing here, sweetie?"

"Jesus," Anna said steadily, her eyes watching me like a hawk. "Jesus," she repeated, giving her head a curt nod.

Jesus? This wasn't going to be easy. I could hardly dismiss Jesus without some explanation. But Anna spoke only a few words. How would I make her understand that this Nativity was not a plaything? It was purely for decorative purposes.

"Oh! So Sunshine is Baby Jesus?"

Anna shook her head. "Jesus," she said again, this time with passion.

I stared dumbly at the doll. If Sunshine wasn't Baby Jesus, then I hadn't a clue. "Well, look, Anna," I coaxed, "Mommy and Daddy are expecting company tonight. I don't think Sunshine should be in here. OK?"

Clearly, she was puzzled, upset. Her lips puckered. Not thrilled, she took the doll and disappeared around the corner, leaving me staring after her in silent wonder and feeling terribly guilty. Had I become too caught up in decorating for the holidays? What was my motive? Unwilling to answer the questions, I cast them furtively to the back of my mind.

Early next morning, I paused reflectively at the Nativity. A pinkish strip of sun streamed through the window, casting a rosy hue over the face of the Christ Child. And there, in front of the stable—to my dismay—lay Sunshine, one eye opened, one eye closed. "Anna, please come here," I called, perturbed.

She toddled in, tiny feet peeking out from under a

polka-dotted gown. I pointed to the doll. "It would really be nice, sweetheart, if you'd just keep Sunshine away from the Nativity," I said. "You might accidentally knock it over." Not a lie, I reasoned.

"Jesus," she said, her eyes pleading.

Obviously she had gleaned a message from the Christmas story; one I must be missing. Again, I had to ask myself what motivated me. Did I want my daughter to understand this blessed season or just fill my house with festive ornaments, hoping to excite my holiday guests? Sobering questions.

Stooping down, I pulled Anna close, determined to get to the bottom of this. "Why do you keep putting Sunshine here, sweetheart? You say she's not Baby Jesus . . ."

She shook her head.

"Well . . ."

"For Jesus," she said haltingly.

"For Jesus," I mumbled under my breath, desperate to understand.

Wiggling from my hold, Anna marched straight for the three wise men and pointed to their gifts. "Oh, I see!" I said, the truth sinking in. "Sunshine is *your* gift to Baby Jesus. Like the wise men. Right?"

Her face beaming like the Virgin Mary's, she nodded, contented. I looked long and hard at Sunshine's exhausted body. Not a pretty gift at all. A definite liability to the creche. Yet when I gazed into my Anna's shining face, I realized she had relinquished her most prized possession—the thing dearest to her heart. My child had captured the true meaning of Christmas, giving sacrificially to her Lord, just as He gave to the world on that first Christmas night.

Suddenly, my hands felt empty, my heart heavy. What gift had I brought to this holy gathering?

I looked down at the cardboard Nativity; the Christ Child looked back at me. In that moment, more than ever before, I knew the only gift He wanted was me. All of me.

Anna bent to take the doll away. "No," I said decisively. "She can stay."

I thought of the stirring words in Phillips Brooks' carol: "O holy Child of Bethlehem, / Descend to us, we pray; / Cast out our sin, and enter in— / Be born in us today."

In the pink light of heaven, I knelt at my daughter's modest shrine and felt a chubby hand gently pat my back. "For Jesus," she whispered, apparently thrilled with her winning explanation. Only now she did not know she spoke the silent prayer of her mother: *For Jesus*. It wasn't a doll I laid at His feet, but a repentant heart.

"Mine eyes have seen thy salvation."
(Luke 2:30, KJV)

You come to us, Lord, again and again. Today, we'll open the door.

*Use what talents you possess: The woods would be very silent if
no birds sang except those that sang best.*
Henry Van Dyke

Fires in
the Night

At the end of a cold and rainy day, I retreated
to the sofa with a steaming cup of chocolate
and my grandmother's scrap quilt. As the
night shadows closed in at the windows, a
fire crackled in the fireplace, casting an orange hue over the
room. Its warmth reached out to me, but the chill in my heart
remained untouched.

For three months, I had not sat down at my desk to write.
Not one single word. After five years of freelancing, I had certainly encountered my share of writer's block and rejection letters, but this time it was something more: I was thinking about
giving it up for good. While God had blessed me with a certain
amount of success, I was growing weary with the struggle, even
doubting my abilities. Maybe I had nothing more to offer. Maybe
it was time to call it quits.

And so, for three months, I had. But I had also been enclosed
in an awful pit of chaotic darkness. Some nights I tossed and

turned till dawn. While words and phrases formed in my head, I refused to get up and write them down. Yet, like a quarrelsome child, the words demanded to be heard; they would not leave me alone.

As I watched the fire's flames lick the stack of oak logs, I was struck by a bizarre thought: *What would happen if I lit a match to my desk? The computer, files, books, everything. Would anybody notice?*

The daunting voices in my head—those I'd contended with for three months—answered me quickly. "Not one person would notice—or care," they assured me.

Deliberately, I rose from the couch and phoned Cindy, a friend in New Jersey. I knew if anybody could cheer me up, she and her undying belief in my abilities could. Immediately, she sensed my mood. "You sound depressed, friend." (She has a pleasant habit of calling me that.)

"Yes, I am depressed," I told her. "I am so depressed I'm considering starting a bonfire with my desk."

She laughed at first, but then she got serious. "Dayle," she said, concerned, "how can you even think about such a thing? You don't want to destroy the gift God has given you."

We talked a long while, and by the time our conversation ended, I felt better but still unsure.

The flames in the fireplace burned low now. The room had grown cold and dim, chilling me to the bone. I walked over to stoke the fire. When I did, flames shot up instantly, flooding the room with hot red colors. I had stoked the fire in this manner hundreds of times before, but this night, the flames held a clear message: *Fire left alone will soon burn out, but stir it up, and it becomes a powerful source of light and warmth.*

As the fire roared, I took great comfort in the message it brought. I knew Cindy was right. The gift of God was surely still in me, just waiting to be rekindled.

Armed with a new sense of purpose, I marched into my office, switched on the lamp, and wrote the story you just read.

"Stir up the gift of God, which is in thee."
(2 Timothy 1:6, KJV)

Father, may I never allow the gift You gave me to turn into ashes.